Advance Praise for I Qui
And Find Your

"I've had the privilege of witnessing countless individuals navigate the challenging waters of career transitions, and *I Quit! How to Lose Your Job and Find Your Dream Career* is the perfect guide for anyone standing at that crossroads. The stories in this book are authentic, heartfelt, and incredibly relatable, each one a testament to the resilience of the human spirit. This collection of journeys isn't just about leaving a job; it's about stepping into purpose, embracing reinvention, and creating a life that aligns with your passions and values. I can't recommend it enough to anyone who's ready to stop settling and start thriving. Veni Folta has masterfully brought together inspiring voices from around the world to remind us that every setback can be a launchpad for something greater. If you're ready to transform your life, this book will be your trusted companion."

Patty Aubery
President, The Canfield Training Group and
NY Times bestselling author and Transformational Leader

"This beautifully curated collection is a powerful reminder that happiness can flourish when we align work with our soul's purpose. A true beacon of happiness, Veni Folta empowers female corporate leaders around the world to transform their careers into joyful, purpose-driven journeys."

Marci Shimoff
#1 NY Times bestselling author of *Happy for No Reason* and
Chicken Soup for the Woman's Soul

"*I Quit! How to Lose Your Job and Find Your Dream Career* brilliantly shows how true wealth isn't found in money alone but in happiness and a career that makes your heart smile. By following these stories, readers learn that happiness and prosperity come naturally when we choose a career that aligns with our hearts."

Ken Honda
International bestselling author of *Happy Money* and *True Wealth*

"The inspiring journeys in *I Quit! How to Lose Your Job and Find Your Dream Career* reveals how career transitions can lead to profound shifts in consciousness and fulfillment. Veni Folta has curated these stories to remind us that true career transformation is rooted in a commitment to one's own inner alignment."

Dr. Jeffery A. Martin
World-renown wellbeing researcher and author of *The Finders*

"With heart and vision, Veni Folta has meticulously put together an anthology that encourages readers to embrace change as a pathway to fulfillment and resilience. *I Quit! How to Lose Your Job and Find Your Dream Career* highlights that aligning career choices with fundamental wellbeing leads to a richer, more meaningful life journey."

Rod Pennington
Founder, Fundamental Wellbeing Foundation and Author of *The Fourth Awakening*

"A key turning point was the 'potato moment,' that set Veni Folta on a path to reinvention, where she embraced mindfulness, positive psychology, and the science of neuroplasticity to heal and redefine her purpose. Veni reminds us to prioritize our health and well-being, and to never stray from our values and passions. Her story is a reflection of her successful transition from corporate leader to a keynote speaker, trainer and life coach dedicating herself to helping others find clarity and purpose in their life journeys. Her story is inspirational and reminds us that every challenge holds the potential for life reinvention and fulfillment."

Maria Mantoudakis
British Telecom Client Lead and Bestselling author of *Tsunami to Greatness*

"*I Quit! How to Lose Your Job and Find Your Dream Career* is a true guide for anyone at a turning point. This book celebrates resilience and purpose, guiding readers to embrace new opportunities with confidence and heart. Through heartfelt stories and powerful insights, Veni Folta guides us to reimagine career transitions with courage and clarity."

Colleen O'Grady, MA. LPC
Author of *Dial Down the Drama* and *Dial Up the Dream*

"I am genuinely moved by the message in *I Quit! How to Lose Your Job and Find Your Dream Career.* This book brilliantly captures the courage and resilience needed to transition toward a career that truly resonates with one's values—a journey I've witnessed countless times in students and colleagues alike. For anyone at a career crossroads, it offers not only inspiration but also actionable wisdom for discovering and pursuing work that deeply fulfills."

Linda D. Rose, EdD
Podcast host, "I Can Do This Show Me How"
Retired President of Santa Ana College & Los Angeles Southwest College

"With 19 inspiring stories of people who turned challenges into opportunities, *I Quit! How to Lose Your Job and Find Your Dream Career* is a powerful catalyst for anyone ready to step into a more purposeful life. I highly recommend this book to anyone seeking to create a career and life they love."

Dr. Wesley Williams, D.C.
Owner, Pioneer Chiropractic

"Drawing on real-world stories of resilience and purpose, *I Quit! How to Lose Your Job and Find Your Dream Career* is an inspiring guide for anyone at a career junction. This book resonates with the message I champion every day: embracing change and understanding that our setbacks can lead to profound growth and transformation. I'm honored to support a work that encourages readers to pursue careers that truly reflect their values and aspirations."

Dr. Connie McReynolds
Author of *Solving the ADHD Riddle* and
Founder of Morningstar Educational and Psychological Services, Inc.

"This book is a guide to discovering joy and abundance by embracing each career shift as a gift of transformation. With deep insight and compassion, Veni Folta has crafted a powerful collection that inspires readers to turn challenges into new beginnings. Enjoy your journey."

Jan Fraser
Author of the bestselling *Jan Fraser Inspired Life Series* books.

I QUIT!
HOW TO LOSE YOUR JOB AND FIND YOUR DREAM CAREER

VENI FOLTA, MBA

Stories by 19 Transformational Thought Leaders from around the world

www.globaltransformation.life/lose-job-find-dream-career-book
For Speaking Engagements or Distribution, contact:
support@globaltransformation.life

Paperback ISBN: **979-8-9921576-1-1**
Hardcover ISBN: **979-8-9921576-2-8**
eBook ISBN: **979-8-9921576-3-5**

Acknowledgements
Publisher: The Inspired Action Group, LLC.
Cover design: Tam Patane, Gwen Medved, and Earl Waud
Website Designer: Tam Patane
Edited by: Tam Patane, Veni Folta, Earl Waud, and Stacey Brown

Printed in the United States of America

This book is dedicated to anyone who's ever faced career challenges and transitions, and are striving to build a career that aligns with their deepest values and dreams.

And to Mama, you were my first inspiration to forge my own path. I hold your love, courage and resilience in my heart and soul, each and every day.

ACKNOWLEDGEMENTS

My heartfelt gratitude goes out to the other eighteen extraordinary authors who have come together to make this book a reality. Each of you has brought a unique story of resilience, courage, and transformation, enriching this collection with your wisdom and experiences. Your willingness to share your journeys has turned this book into a guiding light for anyone seeking purpose and fulfillment in the face of career change.

As our mentor Jack Canfield reminds us, "No one ever climbed Mount Everest without support." This project has been our Everest, and with your collaboration, commitment, and heart, the book came together in record time. Your trust, passion, and dedication to making a difference in the lives of our readers made this climb possible.

A special thank you to Gwen Medved and Tam Patane, who designed the beautiful cover that captures the heart of this book, and to Leona Burton and Stacey Brown, whose expertise and support helped guide us through the publishing process. And to Earl Waud, whose skills and dedication bring the final touches to this volume. Your contributions have added a layer of creativity and professionalism that brings our shared vision to life. And to Jill Eggebraaten and Andrea Sinner for being the Charity Co-chairs who coordinate our charity support efforts.

I am deeply honored to have shared this journey with each of you. Together, we have created something truly special that I know will inspire and uplift others for years to come. Thank you for helping bring this vision to life.

CONTRIBUTING AUTHORS

Leona Burton
Zen Cryar DeBrücke
Terry Deakin
Jill Eggebraaten
Veni Folta
Ryoko Fukui
Kelli Harding
Rhonda Hunt
Linda Jensen
Julie Kelly
John Taylor McEntire
Gwen Medved
Vickie Menendez
Denisa Říha Palečková
Tam Patane
Harish Rao
Leonie Rosenstiel
Andrea Sinner
Earl Waud

Reprinted with Permissions

CONTENTS

Jack Canfield

Jack Canfield is known as America's #1 Success Coach, is a bestselling author, professional speaker, trainer, and entrepreneur. He is the founder and CEO of the Canfield Training Group, which trains entrepreneurs, educators, corporate leaders, and motivated individuals on how to accelerate the achievement of their personal and professional goals.

He has conducted live training for more than a million people in more than 50 countries around the world. He holds two Guinness World Record titles and is a member of the National Speakers Association's Speaker Hall of Fame.

FOREWORD

by Jack Canfield

Co-Creator of the best-selling *Chicken Soup for the Soul*® series
Co-Author of *The Success Principles*™*: How to Get from Where You Are to Where You Want to Be*

I'm thrilled to share these pages with you because I know firsthand the power of reinvention—and how life's biggest obstacles can become our greatest teachers. When I started my career as a high school teacher in inner city Chicago, I wanted to make a difference in the lives of my students. But I quickly realized they needed more than academic lessons. They needed life skills, confidence, and a vision of what was possible for them. That was the seed that set me on a path I hadn't originally planned, yet one that eventually led me to teach, write, and speak about the very principles of success and self-empowerment you'll encounter in this book.

As I began sharing ideas like taking 100% responsibility for your life and your results, setting clear and measurable goals, and utilizing the power of affirmation and visualization, I saw my students start to believe in themselves and their futures. I knew I was on to something important. It wasn't long before I transitioned from teaching in the classroom to sharing these principles with teachers, parents, and, later, with people in all walks of life around the world. This shift led me to write *The Success Principles*™ and launch a career that allowed me to help others transform their lives. I never would have imagined back in those early days that a small pivot toward what I felt passionate about could lead to the work I'm doing now. Yet it did, and it has been the most rewarding decision of my life.

The stories in this book highlight a similar spirit of transformation. Each of the authors here faced a moment that changed their lives—a job loss, a career pivot, or a need to break free from an unfulfilling path.

They chose to step into uncertainty, take responsibility for their outcomes, and committed to creating a life that is aligned with their true purpose. Like my own journey from teacher to author, speaker, and trainer, they took their challenges and turned them into fuel for their future.

One of my core Success Principles, *take 100% responsibility for your life*, is at the heart of each of these stories. When you commit to full responsibility, you recognize that you are the author of your life. You may not control what happens to you, but you do control how you respond. When I left my teaching career to follow my passion for helping others discover their potential, I didn't know exactly where it would take me. But I knew that by taking ownership of my choices and staying open to new opportunities, I could create something meaningful and impactful. That's the choice these authors made too. Rather than letting setbacks define them, they chose to see those moments as opportunities to redefine their lives on their own terms.

The world has shifted dramatically in recent years, with the pandemic sparking a global re-evaluation of what matters most. The "Great Resignation" isn't just about people leaving jobs; it's about people choosing work that resonates with who they are. Millions are stepping away from traditional roles to pursue paths that align with their values, passions, and dreams. The authors of this book are no exception. They saw their career transitions not as losses but as opportunities to pursue work that brought them fulfillment, purpose, and joy.

These stories aren't just personal victories; they're also examples of how personal transformation can ripple out to positively impact others. In that spirit, the authors have chosen to donate the proceeds from this book to support humanitarian causes, including helping the communities affected by the recent Hurricanes Helene and Milton in the United States. The book is a testament to the power of stepping into one's purpose and using that purpose to make a meaningful difference.

As you read, let these stories be a reminder that setbacks are often setups for something greater. Career transitions, job loss, and unexpected changes can be invitations to reconnect with what matters most, to redefine success in a way that feels authentic and inspiring. Just as my journey shifted from teaching students to teaching the world about success, you, too, have the power to reimagine what your future could be.

Taking 100% responsibility doesn't mean you have to figure it all out at once; it simply means committing to your journey, staying open to what's possible, and choosing to believe that your next chapter holds something wonderful.

Let this book be both a guide and a source of encouragement. The authors here have shown that when you trust in yourself, take ownership of your life, and embrace the unknown, you create a life that is more meaningful, more fulfilling, and more aligned with who you truly are. I hope their stories inspire you to take that next courageous step toward *your* dreams.

With love and encouragement,

Jack Canfield

Preface

Have you picked up this book because you too are seeking something more? Are you perhaps at a career crossroads, considering a move toward something more fulfilling? Or maybe you're on the verge of creating your own path, trading traditional employment for work that nourishes your soul? You might even be facing an unexpected job loss and searching for inspiration to guide your next steps.

In the aftermath of the pandemic, the world experienced a seismic shift known as the "Great Resignation," touching every corner of the globe—from the United States and Canada to Europe, to the United Kingdom and the Caribbean. Burnout, the pursuit of more meaningful work, and the re-evaluation of life priorities led millions of workers to step back and ask: **"Is this truly what I want?"** In the process, many discovered that fulfillment and purpose mattered more than traditional notions of job stability. As a result, we've seen a surge in entrepreneurship, career pivots, and roles that align with personal values and aspirations.

Beneath the surface of this movement lies a deeper challenge—a growing, silent pandemic of global mental health struggles that calls for a major shift within our communities. The values, goals, and ambitions we once saw as the keys to a happy life have shifted. Overwork, stress, loneliness, and job insecurity have intensified, creating a profound crisis that demands our attention and action.

In this groundbreaking book, we've gathered the inspiring stories of 19 authors from the United States, Canada, Europe, the United Kingdom, and the Caribbean. These thought leaders from various fields share how they faced job loss, transitions, and personal challenges, yet emerged with renewed or entirely new career paths and life goals. Among them are successful professionals in medicine, law and human resources, corporate leaders, speakers, coaches, entrepreneurs, and "mom-preneurs." Each one, beyond their titles, is a dedicated transformational thought leader with a unique journey of resilience, reinvention, and hope that they want to share with the world.

Their stories are not the typical rags-to-riches narratives, nor are they filled with fairy-tale endings. Rather, their journeys embody the spirit of the Japanese proverb: *"Fall down seven times, stand up eight."*

Some of these authors had a clear vision of their dream careers and meticulously crafted strategies to reach their goals. Others lost their jobs and embarked on an unexpected voyage of self-discovery, discovering passions they either had long forgotten or didn't know that they had. And then there are those who, through chance, stumbled into roles that brought unforeseen joy and fulfillment. Their experiences remind us that success often comes from being open to new opportunities and embracing the unexpected.

Whether you are at the top of your game and considering walking away, knowing at your core that you have more value to give beyond what you have already achieved, or you've been blindsided by an unexpected layoff, or perhaps stuck in a role that has lost its luster, or simply enduring a job you can't stand for the sake of a paycheck—these stories will resonate. They remind us all that it's okay to pivot, to redefine success on our own terms, and to follow multiple passions that enrich our lives.

In fact, you don't even have to walk away from your current job to create meaningful change. Instead, you can reimagine it, shaping your job into a career—or even a calling—that resonates deeply with you.

Putting this book together has been one of the most meaningful projects of my career. What you hold in your hands is more than just a collection of stories—it's a testament to the power of resilience, transformation, and the human spirit. Like me, the authors in this book have experienced job loss and found themselves on unexpected paths to success. But what makes this book even more meaningful is our commitment to giving back. This book came together in record time as we were racing together to get this book published in weeks, not years, so proceeds from the book sale can be raised to support humanitarian causes. By purchasing this book, you will be supporting our first initiative, Project Number One, that benefits the recent victims of Hurricanes Helene and Milton in the United States.

I Quit! How to Lose Your Job and Find Your Dream Career began as my personal journey of career reinvention, as I sought to respond to a deeper calling: to use my own setbacks and triumphs as a beacon of hope to help guide those who want to chart their own course. What started as my individual quest has blossomed into a collaborative project with the amazing, heart-centered authors featured in this book.

This project is a true full-circle moment for me. After losing my first job in Florida because of Hurricane Andrew, I never could have imagined that, decades later, I would be helping others affected by hurricanes through my work. It's a powerful reminder that every challenge we face has the potential to lead us toward something greater.

May these stories inspire you to break free from the stigma of guilt and shame surrounding job loss and career transitions. May they help you see that job loss is not an end, but a beginning stepping stone to something greater. In crisis lies opportunity, and you hold the power to take the next inspired action toward your dreams.

Keep in mind, purposeful intention is everything. You don't need to have all the answers; you just need the courage to ask the right questions, to make decisions and to trust the process. This journey is yours to walk, and you are the author of your own story.

With Deep Love and Gratitude,

Veni Folta
October 10, 2024 - World Mental Health Day

FINDING HAPPINESS

Veni Folta

With 30 years of global senior management experience and over a decade of research and personal practice in neuroscience, cognitive science, positive psychology, and mindfulness meditation, Veni Folta helps high-performing women build a career they love. Specializing in cutting-edge, science-based strategies in an immersive and transformative experience, Veni guides women leaders to rewire their brains and unlock their full potential for career advancement. The women who have worked with Veni experience career growth deeply aligned with their values, purpose, and sense of fulfillment and joy. They don't just succeed professionally—they thrive in every area of their lives.

For information on Veni's keynote speaking, corporate training and executive coaching programs, contact her at:

veni@globaltransformation.life
www.linkedin.com/in/venifolta
www.globaltransformation.life

How I Stumbled upon Happiness – My Long-Term Evolution

By Veni Folta

"The purpose of life is to discover your gift.
The work of life is to develop it.
The meaning of life is to give your gift away." —David Viscott

The Genesis of my Happiness Transformation

Thirty years in the telecom industry taught me a valuable lesson: "long-term evolution" is not only necessary but inevitable.

The most challenging trials we face, while painful, often serve as stepping stones toward who we are destined to become. Reflecting on the past, I realize that each time I lost a job, it was not an end but a new beginning—an opportunity to evolve and push forward on my journey toward the life I truly want to live.

You may recall hearing the term "4G" in older TV commercials, but in the wireless industry, "4G" is known as "Long-Term Evolution" (LTE). LTE represents the fourth generation of wireless technology, preceding the rise of 5G. Despite the current buzz around 5G, LTE remains widely in use across the globe, serving as the critical foundation upon which 5G networks are built.

Remarkably, my career trajectory parallels the evolution of the different generations of wireless technology. When I landed my first job at Sprint, the wireless industry was in its infancy. Barely first generation.

At the time, I had just been laid off by a Japanese company headquartered in Florida. As a young professional, I had been living the dream: managing the company's U.S. operations, flying first class, and living in a beautiful condo on a golf course. My life felt glamorous and secure. I thought my career success was locked in.

But that's the thing about life, it changes, often without warning.

In the pre-dawn hours of one fateful August day in 1992, the most destructive hurricanes in U.S. history hit South Florida. Hurricane Andrew was a one-in-a-century event. It became the first of the costliest and most damaging hurricanes ever to make landfall in the continental United States.

After the 16-foot storm surge receded, I discovered a boat tangled in the mangled branches of a tree in a neighborhood near Coconut Grove. Once the power was restored, images from a housing development in Homestead flashed across the news. Every house on my TV screen had been flattened, blown apart as if a bomb had detonated in that brand-new subdivision.

Although my condo survived, the beachfront property my company had invested millions in for luxury condos was completely destroyed. Disheartened by the loss, the president decided to shut down the office. And just like that, I was out of a job.

In the aftermath of the hurricane, I learned how transient and fragile life can be. Losing my job stripped away the illusion of security and stability, but it also gave me the gift of time. A time to reflect and to re-evaluate what I truly wanted from life.

My husband and I took a break from the corporate world and traveled to Australia and New Zealand. For three months, we roamed the world down under, living out of backpacks and meeting fellow travelers from all over the world. It was during this journey that I realized I wanted a career that would allow me to travel and build relationships across cultures. International business became my beacon.

Entering the World of Telecom: First Generation

When we returned to the U.S., I spotted a job in a newspaper ad for a position at the Fortune 100 telecommunications company Sprint. The role seemed exciting assisting the regional director with a strategic international initiative. I walked into the golden skyscraper for my interview with butterflies in my stomach, eager to start a new chapter.

But when I arrived, I discovered the job was essentially that of an executive assistant.

At first, I hesitated. I had just been managing a Japanese company's U.S. headquarters—how could I justify taking what seemed like a step backward? But the regional director saw my potential and promised to promote me within six months if I helped him launch the initiative. Eager for new opportunities, I took a leap of faith.

Six months later, my mentor had left the company, and the promotion I had hoped for never materialized. I found myself working under a new director, and the environment became increasingly toxic. Realizing I needed a change, I applied for an open sales position, not knowing that this decision would be the turning point that would transform my career.

With the guidance of my new sales manager, I consistently exceeded my quotas and quickly became the go-to person for international business development. My fluency in multiple languages and global perspective helped me build strong relationships with international clients. I became a regular at international Chambers of Commerce events, further expanding my network. Within a year, I earned a spot on Sprint's West Area Vice President Advisory Board, where I worked closely with senior leadership. This prestigious role put me at the table with senior leaders of the company, offering my first real insight into what it was like to collaborate with top executives in the C-suite.

I stayed with the company, but eventually, the urge to explore new horizons returned, reigniting my passion for international business outside of the U.S. mainland.

Moving to a Tropical Island Paradise: Second Generation

The move across the Pacific Ocean put me on track to the next evolution of the wireless industry: 2G. I relocated to Saipan, a remote island paradise in the western Pacific, to work with a small subsidiary of GTE.

With my exemplary telecom sales experience I gained in the U.S. mainland, I was soon tapped by the Network Engineering team to be the subject matter expert from the Sales Department to attend their weekly meetings. We discussed potential network upgrades and buildout, and I provided my sales forecast to ensure we were on target. This opportunity gave me a deeper understanding of the company's operations and the rapidly evolving telecom landscape.

Each year, I found myself landing more clients, driving larger revenues, and cashing bigger commission checks. The adrenaline rush of success became addictive, fueled by the dopamine hit of a growing bank account. Over-delivering quickly became my trademark, both in the office and with my clients. Despite my achievements, once again, I fell into the comforting trap of false security.

If I hadn't realized it then, I certainly understand it now—volatility is inevitable in any emerging industry, and telecom was no exception. Just months before the dot-com bubble burst, I received an email from corporate headquarters announcing a merger with another major telecom company, aiming to create one of the world's premier communications giants in the increasingly competitive local, national, and global markets.

The Dot-com Bubble: Third Generation

As a result of the merger, our local office was earmarked for divestiture and to be sold to the highest bidder. Seeing the inevitable, I knew I needed to act quickly and secured a position with the largest wireless company in the region, based on the neighboring island of Guam.

That was when 3G technology made its debut on the islands, and my career advanced alongside it. I was appointed to lead one of the most exciting growth areas for the company and the wireless industry: international roaming.

For several years, while my children were still very young, I would leave our home in Saipan on Monday or Tuesday, commute on a short flight to Guam for work, and return on the last flight each Friday afternoon. My days were packed with meetings, emails, and calls, leaving me exhausted by the time I got home. During this period, I also began attending—and hosting—international conferences with major wireless partners from Asia, the United States, Europe, and beyond. This was when I really hit my stride to become the corporate road warrior that I was for almost two decades.

As my career catapulted, so did the demands of my job. I started to neglect my well-being—skipping meals, ignoring bathroom breaks, and surviving on just a few hours of sleep each night. What began as occasional back pain soon became chronic, and my energy levels plummeted. Yet, driven by my passion for the work and my connection with colleagues from around the world, I continued pushing forward, convincing myself that sacrifice was the price of success.

It wasn't until my health reached a breaking point that I realized how unsustainable my lifestyle had become.

The First Wake-Up Call: Cancer

It was a terrifying moment when I was diagnosed with cancer, one that forced me to confront the reality that I had been neglecting my health for far too long. I underwent surgery, and thankfully, the cancer was caught early enough to be removed, and I was cancer-free. But the experience left me shaken, especially when another colleague who had the same cancer diagnosis passed away six months later. I broke down at her funeral when I realized that her two young children were the same ages as mine. The thought that I could have been the one lying in that casket, and what that would have meant for my family was harrowing. It was a sobering reminder of what was at stake.

I tried to slow down, focusing more on my health and my family, but the corporate demands didn't relent. Old habits die hard, and before long, I was back to working long hours and traveling constantly. I told myself that I could handle it, that I was strong enough to manage it all. But I was wrong.

My "Potato Moment": A Life on the Brink

One late afternoon, I found myself standing in the kitchen, peeling potatoes while on a conference call with colleagues from the U.S., Korea, and Japan. We were in the middle of negotiating a high-stakes deal, and I was trying to juggle cooking dinner for my kids while managing this critical conversation. My heart was racing, my breath shallow, and I suddenly felt the peeler slip from my hand. It was a small, almost trivial incident, but it felt monumental. I realized at that moment that I was on the brink—trying to balance too much, and I was about to lose it all.

That Sunday, I was at the movie theater with my kids when my silenced cell phone kept buzzing. I was traveling so much at this time and quality time with my kids was rare. "We need you to fill in for Jane at the Mobile World Congress tomorrow in Barcelona," the Senior Vice President's assistant texted me. My boss got sick and couldn't get on the plane. Since I was next in command, I had to go as her backup.

I looked at my daughters who just wanted some time with their mom, and knew I would have to break the disappointing news to them. I was already scheduled to fly to Korea later that week for a critical deal, so I changed my ticket to fly directly from Spain to Korea, skipping the trip home. I hastily packed my suitcase that night, with my nine-year-old daughter standing next to me asking, "mom, when are you going to stop traveling?" My heart sank. I could hardly hold back my tears.

The next day, after over 24 hours in transit, I checked into an executive suite at the W overlooking the water before I headed out to the Fira de Barcelona Convention Center for my first meeting. The meetings went on until the evening and by then, I was up almost 36 hours and hadn't eaten a thing. I ordered a salad from room service and crawled into bed. I woke up hours later, the untouched plate still resting on my chest. I had fallen asleep from sheer exhaustion.

From Barcelona, I flew directly to Korea for another round of meetings. By the time I checked into my hotel in Seoul, my body had reached its limit. As I walked to the window to take in the view of the mountains, the world suddenly tilted. I collapsed on the floor.

My body was keeping score and that was its way of telling me that enough was enough.

The Breakdown: A Forced Pause

After years of pushing myself, my body finally gave out. Diagnosed with chronic fatigue and depression, I felt like my world was crumbling. It was devastating. My identity has been tied to my career and to my ability to push through obstacles. But now I was forced to stop. I had to confront the fact that I couldn't continue down this path.

During my recovery, I discovered a book that changed my life: *The Brain That Changes Itself* by Dr. Norman Doidge. The concept of neuroplasticity fascinated me—the idea that I could rewire my brain and change my life. Over the next decade, I immersed myself in the study of neuroscience, cognitive science, positive psychology and mindfulness meditation. Slowly but surely, I began to heal.

The Turning Point: From Corporate Leader to Coach and Mentor

The pandemic gave me another unexpected gift of time. With global business travel halted, I was able to focus on my health and family. I became certified as a "Happy for No Reason" trainer and as a public service, I started offering free webinars for other women from professional organizations to share the science-based tools that had helped me overcome stress and anxiety.

The response from these isolated, socially distanced women was overwhelmingly positive. Many, like me, were already struggling with the challenges of balancing demanding careers with family obligations and personal well-being. With the pandemic underway, they were eager to learn how to regain control of their lives and find a sense of inner peace amid the chaos. I realized my journey—from career setbacks to personal growth and transformation—was not unique. My story resonated deeply with these women, and I knew I had found my calling.

A couple of years after the pandemic ended, due to a reduction in headcount, my position was eliminated after nearly two decades with the same company. But this time, I wasn't afraid. In fact, I had been preparing for this moment. A quote from a European colleague's profile: "We have two lives, the second begins when we realize there is only one worthy of our dreams" became my impetus.

I founded The Inspired Action Group, a business strategy and coaching consultancy dedicated to helping women navigate career transitions and discover their true calling. With my newfound clarity and sense of purpose, I also became a keynote speaker and corporate trainer, sharing my journey and the powerful scientific tools that had helped me turn adversity into opportunity. My message resonated with audiences from all over the world—especially women professionals who, like me, had faced career setbacks and were looking for a way to rebuild and thrive. I had the opportunity to help others on their own journeys of transformation, and it was incredibly fulfilling.

My Long-Term Evolution: 4G, 5G and beyond

I can see clearly now that every setback, every job loss, and every challenge was part of a larger evolution that I wasn't fully aware of at the time. Each experience shaped me, pushing me to grow, to reflect, and to ultimately discover my true purpose. From my early days in the telecom industry, to becoming a corporate road warrior who traveled to fifty countries, worked long hours, and neglected my own needs. To my "potato moment" in the kitchen when I realized I couldn't continue living the way I was. The path has been winding, but it has always led me toward something greater.

Before I decided to leave the wireless industry, I had become one of the industry spokespersons for 4G Long-Term Evolution in international roaming. I was invited to speak on a number of panels at global telecom conferences. As the telecom industry embraces 5G and beyond, my journey evolves alongside it. Just like the message I carry — adapting and growing, yet always rooted in connection and purpose.

Today, I am living my dream. My work is deeply fulfilling, and I feel more aligned with my purpose than ever before.

But more importantly, I've learned the importance of balance, of taking care of myself physically and mentally so that I can show up fully for myself, my family, clients, and community. It's a lesson that took years to learn, and I'm still a work in progress, but it has made all the difference. My journey, from losing jobs to discovering my true calling, has taught me that the most challenging moments are often the ones that shape us the most.

To any woman reading this book who has experienced job loss, burnout, or a sense of being stuck, I want you to know that this is not the end of your story; it's the beginning of a new chapter. Because of our brain's ability to rewire and make new neural pathways, each of us has the capacity for long-term evolution, even if we can't always see it in the moment. The setbacks we face are not failures; they are opportunities for growth and transformation. Trust your ability to evolve, take inspired actions, and know that your best days are ahead.

As I continue my journey, I remain committed to helping others find their way—whether through coaching, speaking, corporate training or the stories in this book. My goal–and I hope my legacy–is to inspire one million people globally, to turn adversity into opportunity and create lives for themselves that are happier, healthier, more fulfilling and filled with purpose.

I invite you to embark on a journey with me to rewire your brain, transform your life, and become part of a thriving community of one million happy, healthy, and fulfilled individuals!

I will leave you with this quote from Confucius that has inspired me on my current path of evolution:

If there is light in the soul,
There will be beauty in the person,
If there is beauty in the person,
There will be harmony in the house,
If there is harmony in the house,

There will be order in the nation,
If there is order in the nation,
There will be peace in the world.

Zen Cryar DeBrücke

Zen Cryar DeBrücke is the founder of Fear Free Human LLC. She has worked with over 40,000 people, helping them align with their purpose and unlock lives of greater fulfillment and joy by showing them how to listen to their Internal Guidance System®.

Her compassion radiates through her work, and her style is down-to-earth, practical, humorous, and wise. Zen's international best-selling book, ***Your Inner GPS*** is an easy-to-read how-to on the way to let this inner wisdom guide you to success. She is a member of the Transformational Leadership Council. Zen Lives in Idaho and founded the Fear Free Human Movement, an international best-selling author, breast cancer survivor, happy wife, and busy mom.

Contact z@fearfreehuman.com
fearfreehuman.com
IG: Fearfreehuman

Feeling My Way into Happiness and Success

By Zen Cryar DeBrücke

"Everything is going to be ok. If it's not ok then it's not over." —John Lennon

When I was a child, life was anything but predictable or safe. We lived out in the country; in a home my parents had built with their own hands. It took them two and a half years to complete, and the strain on the family was intense. This isolated life, which should have brought peace, became a pressure cooker of unresolved tensions. I grew up surrounded by arguments, anger, and often physical abuse from my mom, who had nowhere to vent her frustration. I would lie in bed, feeling trapped, powerless, and dreaming of escaping a life dictated by others' anger.

One of my mother's escapes was her nightly ritual of watching Dynasty or Dallas, which offered a world so different from the one I knew. I remember sneaking out of bed and crawling on my belly like a little carpet commando on a mission. Down the hall, I'd go to watch the glamor from behind the end table, crammed between the wall and the couch. There, hidden and barely breathing, I would watch the confident, powerful women on the screen navigate their worlds with poise and control. One character captivated me—she stood, clad in her strong, shoulder-padded, business attire, declaring her intent to lead her company despite the men's resistance and disbelief. It struck something deep in me. It felt expansive and right. I didn't fully understand it, but I knew I wanted to be like her, but more than being like her, I wanted to do what she was doing. I wanted to run a company and be a CEO, whatever that was. The thought filled me with excitement, energy, and, for the first time, a spark of a real future.

In the following years, I held on to that spark like a lifeline, even as life challenged me. I had no idea what running a company was all about; no one in my family had ever run one. It was a feeling inside more than an actual strategy.

When I turned seventeen, I could no longer bear the life I was in. I sued my father for emancipation, dropped out of high school, and struck out on my own, determined to escape the patterns of abuse and rage that had defined my upbringing. But I hadn't realized then that these patterns weren't just tied to my family, they had become ingrained in me now. Every disappointment and every frustration were met with the same explosive anger I'd seen growing up. I lost jobs, alienated friends, and found myself in a cycle of self-sabotage. All the feelings I had left home to escape were now mine being carried with me.

Then, a friend gave me a cassette tape by Abraham Hicks. The tape talked about the Law of Attraction, and my thinking was the problem, not the situations I found myself in. Skeptical but desperate, I listened to the tape over and over. The interviewer asked me a profound question: "How do we have the most successful and happy life?" It was a simple question, but the answer changed my life. She said that each person has an "internal guidance system" that helps them stay aligned with their best path. When a person's thoughts are in alignment, they feel an opening sensation in the body. When they're misaligned, they feel a sense of tightness or contraction. I realized then that I had been ignoring these signals all my life. Every time I'd blown up, stormed out, or made a decision I regretted, I'd felt that constriction in my chest, that tightening sensation. *It would be a few years before I realized that the expanded feeling I felt that night watching the beautiful woman declare she would lead was an opening and part of my perfect path!*

This idea of an inner compass felt like a revelation, a lifeline in the chaos. I searched everywhere to find more information on these sensations. It was right before the internet became public. I called the Hicks, but they had no courses or books yet. I looked in my local library; there was nothing.

I finally realized I was going to have to figure it out for myself. For the first time, I began to pay attention to my body's responses, noticing when I felt open and energized versus closed and tense. Little by little, this internal guidance began to shape my choices. Following that feeling of openness, I quickly completed community college, and then transferred to UC Davis, where I completed a degree in foreign policy. My life began to accelerate and shift in unexpected ways. I started my own export business while at university, which led me to the world of internet technology. I found myself involved in website development through contacts and clients just as the internet was taking off. By the time I was twenty-nine, I had achieved my dream of becoming a CEO. I was running Netkitchen, a thriving web design firm with offices in San Francisco and London, with many Fortune 500 clients. All of this was accomplished by my simply following the opening sensations and not believing in the fear-based closing sensations.

For a while, everything was perfect. I was living the dream that had started in a dark hallway, watching a TV screen from behind the end table. But then my success came crashing down. The dot-com bubble burst, and overnight, everything I had built began to crumble. Our biggest clients pulled back their budgets, projects were shelved, and we soon faced $1.2 million in debt that we had personally guaranteed. My world felt like it was imploding. I was consumed by fear again, drowning in thoughts of failure and self-doubt. I lay awake, night after night, feeling that same tightness in my chest, the feeling I had learned to recognize as misalignment. I knew that fear thinking was guidance to find a new thought that created the opening or expansion feeling, but I could not find one single thought that opened me.

But now, instead of running from it, I listened. My Internal Guidance System® (IGS) was guiding me, reminding me of its presence even in my darkest hour. One night, as I lay there unable to sleep, I decided to test it. "What if," I thought, "this entire experience is meant to teach me something?"

That single thought opened me up a little bit, and then a thought came out of nowhere— "I am earning my experiential MBA?" A wave of expanding calm rippled through the center of my body. For the first time in weeks, I felt an opening, a sense of confidence again. At that moment, I knew I was exactly where I needed to be.

The next day, I walked into the office with renewed purpose. The fear of failure no longer consumed me; I was curious about what this experience could teach me. People noticed the change immediately. They asked if I'd found some miracle solution or new strategy to save the company, and I told them about my IGS, really for the first time. A friend actually said, "Tell us the name of the doctor giving you the drugs or share your secret because we are all a mess, and you're taking this like it's an adventure." I laughed, and I did tell them. "It's this internal guidance system—this Inner GPS I decoded. It's like an internal compass, helping me navigate even these rough waters."

In the following months, the company struggled but survived. The debt was paid off, and I began to understand just how powerful the IGS truly was. It was more than creating a life of happiness; it also created a life of purpose and contribution. I started sharing my experiences, holding small gatherings with friends and colleagues, and showing them how to connect with their own IGS. This tool was more than just a way to feel better; it was a blueprint for living a life free from fear and anxiety. The fear that had once paralyzed me now felt like a helpful signal, a reminder to check in, adjust, and realign with my best path.

As I taught others, the Fear Free Human project was born—a vision of a future where people would learn to live free from mental fear, guided instead by this inner sense of alignment. Over the years, I refined the method, developing exercises to help people tune into the sensations from their IGS, recognize the feeling of openness versus closing, and make choices from that place of inner clarity. I am a student of the Internal Guidance System® as much as I am its teacher, learning from the thousands of people who reached out to share their experiences, their fears, and their breakthroughs.

My journey with the IGS has spanned decades now, and it has touched over 40,000 lives. I have seen people transform, finding peace, purpose, and alignment in ways they never thought possible. This tool has become more than a personal compass; it is a movement, a path forward for those seeking to live authentically, free from the constraints of fear-based decision-making. In my work, I teach that the IGS is not just for navigating crises or major life decisions—it is a daily tool that cultivates joy, health, and connection by consistently tuning into that feeling of openness.

Looking back, I see how every challenge and setback was a part of this journey. My success and subsequent upheaval during the dot-com crash were not accidents but stepping stones, each experience guiding me closer to my true path. The lesson I learned, and now teach, is simple: when we trust our IGS, we discover that life has a natural rhythm, a flow that leads us to exactly where we are meant to be.

As I think about the future, I imagine a world where everyone learns to listen to their IGS—a world where mental fear no longer dictates choices or defines our lives. In my vision, children grow up knowing they have a divine wisdom inside that loves them and holds the wisdom they need to have a beautiful life. They can trust that feeling of openness to guide them to make a more significant contribution to the world. I imagine a classroom 1000 years from now where a child asks, "What does fear feel like?" the teacher responds with a gentle smile, "I don't know. We haven't felt it in many, many generations."

The IGS has brought me here, and my mission now is to share it with as many people as possible. My journey from that dark, cramped hallway to the heights of the tech world, and ultimately to a life dedicated to helping others find freedom from fear, has been a testament to the power of trusting our inner guidance. It's a journey I am grateful for every day and one I know is just beginning. The more people I reach, the more confident I am the Internal Guidance System® is not just a tool for personal transformation—it is a key to a future where we can all live fully, fearlessly, and freely aligned with our best selves.

Kelli Harding

Kelli Harding, MD, MPH, is dedicated to promoting a kinder and healthier world for all. An expert in mental health, medicine, and public health, she teaches at Columbia University in New York City. Dr. Harding authored the acclaimed book *The Rabbit Effect: Live Longer, Happier, and Healthier with the Groundbreaking Science of Kindness.* She appeared on Today, Good Morning America, BBC, and other media. Co-founder of Our Kind of Club, a global community centered on kindness, Dr. Harding has spoken at the United Nations and World Happiness Summits. She lives in NYC with her husband, three sons, and rescue dog, Athena.

Website kellihardingmd.com
www.linkedin.com/in/kellihardingmdmph
Instagram @kellihardingmd

Alchemy of a Calling

By Kelli Harding, MD, MPH

"When you want something, all the universe conspires in helping you to achieve it." —Paulo Coelho

"Every setback and hard-earned lesson becomes part of a transformative education that reveals your greater purpose—that's the alchemy of a calling."

Sitting in the sun on a marble bench in the cool October air, surrounded by swirling yellow leaves and the chatter of birds and students on Columbia University's campus, I reflect on the twists and turns that led me here. Every experience—the highs and the challenges—had its role in bringing me to this moment. My titles and jobs have changed over the years, but my true north emerged clearly–to help people live full, happy, and healthy lives. To get to my current destination, I had to learn to flow with the wind.

Let me backup a bit.

I wanted to be a medical doctor since I was a girl growing up in a small beach town in Northern Florida. My aunt and uncle, both physicians, lived nearby. We got together often, and I loved overhearing their dinnertime stories about mysterious illnesses that they figured out just in time to save a patient's life. And how they noticed small clues, like a curious physical or lab finding, that others had missed to reveal the true diagnosis. I also saw how my aunt and uncle greeted the patients we'd see in town with heartfelt smiles and a mutual, warm admiration. As a kid, life as a doctor seemed to provide the perfect blend of science, kindness, and Sherlock Holmes mystery. I felt determined to have a front-row seat to the human experience and pursue a life in medicine.

But along the path to medical school, I took a detour.

By high school, my parents left Florida's tropical beaches for the desert mountains of northern Nevada. I only saw my aunt and uncle a few times a year, and their evening stories faded under the sun of my new love–writing. Thanks to classes with dedicated public school English teachers, I lost myself in the joyful flow of ideas and the ability to reach another person beyond the page in space and time, much as you and I are connected now.

In my senior year of high school, I applied for and got two internships–one in the fall, working on stories at a local TV station, and one in the spring, volunteering in the local hospital ER. As fall turned to winter, I relished the thrill of jumping in the cozy TV satellite van with the investigative team to document breaking news around town. By December of my senior year, I was doing on-camera interviewing, started editing, and decided to extend my internship through the spring. I forgot about medicine and decided to become a journalist instead.

I studied political science at the University of California, Berkeley, because my mentors said it was a good major for future journalists. I would have continued on that path had it not been for an experience one afternoon during my second year.

Sitting silently in the front row of a big lecture hall, I listened to the hum of the professor discussing comparative politics. The student sitting to my right suddenly slumped in his seat, fell into his desk, and crashed to the floor. Papers flew everywhere as he started convulsing. I instinctively leaped out of my chair to crouch by his side. As students and the professor gathered around, I felt powerless. If you have ever seen a grand-mal seizure, you understand what I mean. Then, in the pause of chaos, a clear dormant desire arose–I wanted to help. As the ambulance sirens grew louder outside, alarms went off internally. I remembered my calling.

That day, I became pre-med.

Over the next several years, I studied diligently and eventually went to medical school to learn everything I could about the human body. Halfway through, when I got to the hospital wards and met the patients, I had the unsettling feeling that something with my understanding of disease wasn't adding up.

The first two years of medical school involve sitting in classrooms and anatomy labs. Everything is very controlled and has an explanation. Then, as a third-year student on the wards, I met the patients and was confronted with the complexity of human life. The mismatch between textbooks and reality was glaring.

At first, I rejected what I saw and longed for clear answers, but then I got hooked by the mystery. What were the hidden factors that contributed to some people defying difficult diagnoses and others suffering so terribly from treatable diseases? The question of why the same illnesses have such different courses in different people fascinated me, and I became a woman on a mission–what were we missing in medicine?

It turned out a lot.

Initially, I thought it had something to do with the mind-body connection, for which no formal course of study existed. So, I forged my own path. After graduating, I first studied internal (adult) medicine, then did a residency in psychiatry. But I still didn't feel I had the answers. Because of that, I did a two-year National Institute of Mental Health research fellowship at Columbia, studying medically unexplained symptoms. Meanwhile, to support myself financially, I worked in the emergency room, seeing patients with medical and psychiatric concerns. That's when something unexpected happened.

I fell in love with a job.

The ER is the wild-west of the hospital. It is loud, messy, and never the same on two given shifts. The beds are tight, and you work quickly and closely with others to solve complex problems. As hard as it was, I looked forward to seeing my colleagues daily. They became like a second family. And you just can't make up the patient stories, especially in New York City. The clientele ranges from straight out of newspaper headlines to naked people found on New York City streets. I often stayed late to take on just one more case. And I then did something I now see as a red flag.

Due to an error in my timesheet, I went unpaid for multiple shifts. After several failed attempts to fix the situation, I let it go and chalked it up to volunteering, even though I needed the money. I told myself I loved my job and was happy to serve despite feeling embarrassed to tell my husband. Plus, I was finally making progress on the medical mystery of why exactly some people do so well with illnesses and others struggle. I got tipped off by some rabbits.

The answer to my question had to do with hidden factors far outside the hospital, factors in our everyday lives like love and kindness.

I saw that it was a huge public health story that needed to be told to people far and wide outside the hospital doors. It led me to enroll in evening classes at Columbia's Mailman School of Public Health and to start formulating an idea for a popular book that would become ***The Rabbit Effect.*** I knew the information could change lives. Meanwhile, things were changing in the ER.

Even before the pandemic, we were understaffed and under-resourced to meet the tremendous needs of the community. There was frequent staff turnover. And in the void, my lovely work partner and I got promotions. The overwhelm was incredible, and he kept having vague physical symptoms he thought were related to job stress. Then, in an instant, the world changed.

My dear friend received a life-altering diagnosis. The next day, he was gone on medical leave. At first, the adrenalin got me through doing both our jobs. And I then got bogged down in grief and the day-to-day exhaustion. We were so short-staffed I didn't want to leave my colleagues hanging. So, I kept showing up and going through the motions. My love of my job turned to depersonalization and chronic overwhelm. When I was offered a further promotion, I turned it down. Looking back, I was experiencing classic burnout. But I couldn't see it until a meeting changed everything.

Confronted with your mortality or a friend's, you start to rethink life and wonder, "What is our purpose here? What's my true mission? Is this enough?" Part of me knew the ideal of medicine and helping people no longer matched up with the day-to-day reality of my job. Then, I got a call out of the blue to meet on the hospital's upper floors, far from the ER. I had no idea what it was about. I remember feeling so sick that day that I'd considered calling in, but I didn't want to burden my colleagues by being short-staffed.

The administrator's office was clean, quiet, and filled with light in stark contrast to the constant beeps and commotion of the windowless ER. I sat, stuffy-nosed, disheveled in scrubs, across from the same man in a fancy suit with perfectly combed hair who had previously offered me a promotion. Only this time, the conversation went differently. He held a paper with numbers to discuss.

My patient statistics showed I wasn't seeing the required number of patients per shift. I wish I could say the conversation was supportive and that he recognized the recent situation, that I often picked up more medically complex patients because of my background, or that I spent extra time talking to patients and families to explain what was happening. These were not the metrics that mattered. Instead, I was informed there would be consequences if my numbers didn't pick up. And then he said something that knocked the wind out of me.

"Maybe you're not cut out for the ER."

His words hung heavy in the air between us. I stared at him. My confusion was akin to a lawyer telling me my partner was filing for divorce. It felt so impersonal. How could a job I'd dedicated so many years to, loved, and sacrificed so much for leave me feeling so betrayed? I suddenly remembered a trusted mentor who told me, "Institutions don't love you back."

After an awkwardly long stare between us, I woke up from my stupor. When I turned the office door handle to leave, I knew it was time to quit. When I later told my husband and friends, they asked, "What took you so long?" As painful as the conversation was, it was the step back I needed to ask myself, "Am I using my unique talents in the way that is the best for me to serve?"

Several months later, after accepting another position, I resigned.

It's strange how things work out. That unwelcome conversation was my mental leap to move on and focus on my bigger mission. Maybe I would have stayed on and remained in the fog of burnout if it hadn't happened.

In the aftermath, I wrote and sold my first book, ***The Rabbit Effect,*** which came out to critical acclaim. It was Fall 2019, and I got to do a ten-city nationwide book tour. Because I had more control over my schedule, I could go. I even took my family with me. It was a dream come true to talk to people across the U.S. about health and happiness and how we can take better care of one another as a nation. And I was finally taking care of myself.

Then 2020 happened.

The ER was tough before the pandemic. And during, it was an absolute nightmare. At the start, we lost my wonderful colleague, Dr.

Lorna Breen, to suicide. She was a great clinician who loved medicine and the ER. It still shakes me. We must take better care of the caregivers before we lose anyone else. I know from firsthand experience that burnout is a common problem, and it can be hard to see the symptoms in yourself. Instead, we can look out for each other. At every talk I give, I imagine Lorna and other lost colleagues sitting in the audience. The journey feels worth it if I help one person feel less alone.

My focus on creating a kinder and healthier world for all has led me to teach on global stages, including national media outlets, World Happiness Summits, and the United Nations. I've joined with people from over 18 countries as part of Our Kind of Club, a global group I co-founded to uplift others with the science of kindness and remind people of our shared humanity in challenging times. Doing this joyful work, I remember who I am and how I can serve.

My love for medicine has evolved and taken on many forms. I still see patients and am deeply honored to support people through life challenges. I also have the joy of teaching Columbia University's next generation of doctors, sharing the science and heart of medicine. And then there's the writing—a chance to reach beyond the hospital to help even more people feel empowered in their health journeys. Unfortunately, our current system is essentially "sick care" rather than true healthcare, often focused on managing crises rather than preventing them. Through my work, I hope to contribute to more people staying healthier longer and avoiding the ER altogether.

Reflecting back, I realize unexpected twists and turns are essential to understanding a calling. Every setback and hard-earned lesson becomes part of a transformative education that reveals your greater purpose—that's the alchemy of a calling. Your struggles and healing are tools to help others. Together, we are part of a much larger picture, and the work doesn't end with any one of us. Our legacy is to inspire each other to keep building a more peaceful, compassionate world. From my work, I know peace is health–and we can create that together.

Remember, you are far more than a job so there's no need to get too attached. In Western culture, we often wrap our identities around our roles, getting caught up in prestige and forgetting who we are beyond work. But titles come and go while life constantly invites us towards something grander – a universal calling. Like the wind, your calling has been a persistent force guiding your life. What are the whispers in the wind that you need to follow? What situations do you need to stop fighting against and instead go with the flow to discover where you are needed most and follow where the universe is guiding you?

May the joy of pursuing a greater purpose fill your days with meaning and love and inspire you to light the way for others.

Denisa Říha Palečková

Denisa Říha Palečková is a leading intimacy and relationship expert with over two decades of experience. A bestselling author and TEDx speaker, she offers innovative perspectives on sexuality, health, and personal development. Denisa has empowered countless individuals and couples to enhance their lives through her acclaimed workshops, retreats, and online programs. As the founder of CORE TOUCH® Holistic Sensual Massage training and the ARKAYA® Body Center, she is recognized internationally for her transformative work in healing and conscious intimacy, helping people lead more joyful and fulfilled lives.

denisapaleckova.com
IG: https://www.instagram.com/denisapaleckova_official
YT: https://www.youtube.com/DenisaRihaPaleckovaENG

Sacred Sexuality and Connecting to Your Creative Core

By Denisa Říha Palečková

"Wherever you go, go with all your heart." —Confucius

My story is not quite as dramatic as losing my job completely. I have been lucky enough never to have to work at something that isn't meaningful to me — in fact, I started my own business when I was still a university student. I was working part-time at a massage studio as a free-lancer, but the experience of being 'fired' gave me a moment of reflection that inspired me to follow my path, a chance that led to more opportunities and deeper insights. It set me on a powerful journey that I've been following for more than 20 years.

It all began back in 1996. I was 20 and in my first long-term relationship, and I had started to wonder: "There must be more to sex than this!" I thought of sex as something very magical, special, and profound, but my experience back then was sort of 'average.' Not bad, but not very good either.

One day, I found a paper flyer advertising "A Taste of Tantra" in a spiritual bookstore, and I thought: "This could help our sex life." I started by attending an evening session, then a weekend and a week-long course. Eventually, I went into a two-year training program. This was really the beginning of this kind of work in my country, the Czech Republic. I was among the first to train in this field, learning massage, sensual massage, and genital massage as part of it.

After I had finished the training, a friend on the course said one of their friends was looking for a Tantra massage therapist for her business club in Prague. I was pretty scared but also curious and courageous, so I thought: "Okay, I'll try it." When I started doing it professionally, I was really touched. I could see how my massage could open up the other person and awaken them to who they really are.

I met a lot of business people, politicians, and especially men who were successful in their careers but unhappy and unfulfilled personally. They were often lonely, even in their marriages, because they were detached from their hearts and from who they truly were. They were living stories that weren't even theirs. And I could see how my touch and approach helped them come back to themselves. Sometimes it came as a shock, like: "How come I'm living a life that isn't meaningful to me?" The shock of realizing you're living a life you don't actually want. When I could see the profound effect this massage had, I started to love it even more because it was helping people get back on track and be happier. This kept me going. Initially, I was rather worried — wondering if this was an erotic business — but then I saw the context and the power of the work I was doing.

I called it tantric massage - but over time, I have developed my own form of sensual holistic massage, which I call CORE TOUCH®. Still, in 2001, this profession was very new to Prague. Now people are very familiar with the concept, but back then, it was just developing. I was working on my own, so I was constantly searching for more training and teachers. In 2003, I found a course in Germany run by the founder of the tantric massage tradition there. In Germany, this profession is well-developed and also legally acknowledged. They have the Tantra Massage Verband, an organization to protect the quality of this profession.

I happened to be training with the owner of a massage studio in Cologne, one of the first professional studios in this field in Germany. She invited me to be part of her team, so it was the first time I could be part of a community in this profession. Since this profession is very particular, working with human intimacy and feelings, I really appreciated the opportunity to talk with other professionals, to learn and grow, and I loved being part of a team. It wasn't a full-time job because I was still teaching my own courses and living in Prague, but every few weeks, I would fly to Cologne to work up to a week in this massage studio.

I was doing what I loved. While it wasn't 100% of my professional life or income, there was inspiration and growth. Then, in 2006, after about two years, something happened at the massage studio that led to my departure. I felt saddened by it, as I would have happily continued there for many more years.

However, being fired gave me more time and space. This change happened at a point when I had already trained other professionals in this kind of massage. I could gradually pass my clients in Prague on to my students because they shared my expertise. Step by step, this organically developed into my opening of a massage studio in 2007. It was called Tantra Spa because I wanted to highlight the wellness aspect, and we still referred to the technique as tantric massage.

Later on, we decided to rename the massage and studio because some people expected a spiritual experience or a cheap erotic massage. We didn't want to attract clients with those kinds of expectations. So, we rebranded as Sensual Holistic Massage under the name CORE TOUCH®, as it reaches deep down to the core of your being. Later, we adopted the name ARKAYA® Body Center. The word "arkaya" in Sanskrit means "to raise your life force," referring to the life energy inside our bodies. The origin of the name came in 2006 at a yoga training session in Los Angeles. I had my journal with me, and when I was going through my notes many years later, I found I had noted it would be a good name for a massage studio.

The essence or purpose of this place is to bring people back to their bodies and hearts. Personally, I have found that learning and growing by experiencing my own body and sensuality was a significant tool for my own transformation. When I was in my twenties, I remember thinking: "There must be more to sex than what I've experienced." It wasn't bad, but it wasn't amazing either. I had this feeling that sex, or making love, should be profound, blissful, and beautiful.

This curiosity led me to join seminars and, later on, a two-year tantric training course run by an English teacher in our country. I was so detached from my body and my feelings in my twenties that I was not even aware of it. Due to this, I couldn't experience anything profound while making love — I was alienated from my very core being.

So sensual bodywork was a turning point in my personal and, later, professional journey. I started translating workshops from English to Czech for many teachers, during which I learned so much, and it also prepared me to speak in front of groups. Then I was asked to co-teach a workshop, and eventually, I began to teach couples' and women's workshops; while for the first few years, it was just a hobby that offered some pocket money, it developed gradually into a tangible income resource. Until today, conscious work with the body and sexuality is the main aspect of my work, whether it's through couples' and women's workshops, or courses for both men and women.

Grounding in our own body is where we are most vulnerable and where as a society, most of us are wounded when it comes to our sexuality. We are trained to feel shame for our bodies and how we look, to feel ashamed of our sexual feelings and needs. We are afraid to communicate how we feel, and we hesitate to set boundaries or communicate our desires. I see this constantly, even in couples who have been together for 30 years. They tell me, "We only ever had sex but never talked about it." In couples' workshops, they often start talking about their intimate life for the first time.

As a teacher and motivational speaker in this field, I observe how uneducated we are in terms of our bodies and sexuality and how much wounding, taboo, shame, and unexpressed feelings there are. People also carry real trauma from sexual abuse, difficult childbirth, medical procedures, and the scarring that follows. Wounding doesn't need to be related to sexuality — childhood wounds manifest too. This is what arises in both the seminars and the massage studio. I was fortunate not to be part of any corporate experience that wasn't meaningful to me. Being fired from someone else's business propelled me on my journey to creating my own massage studio in 2007. I love being able to send clients from my courses for individual work there.

It's not just about experiencing massage but reconnecting with oneself — our feelings, our heart, our body. People learn to trust that they can express how they feel and be received and appreciated. They also release unexpressed emotions that they've held back in an attempt to be normal and functional.

In the studio, there's the space to be educated on touch, massage, and understanding our bodies, sexuality, sensuality, needs, and boundaries. It's very much needed in our society. We may seem sexually free because of the huge pornography industry, but we are far from it — in fact, we are very restricted in our sexuality.

My aim is to bring back the perception of sexual energy as something pure, natural, and sacred. Sexual energy is the creation energy — it's what gives life. It can be used in many ways, and when we are connected to our bodies and sexuality, we are more powerful, intuitive, creative, and self-aware. Being grounded in our bodies gives us clarity about who we are, what we want, and what we don't want.

Especially for women, healthy sexuality — being connected to this life force — makes one more self-aware. It's not about being in a couple or having a sexual partner; it's about being connected to the power within. A relaxed, alive pelvis brings more profound self-awareness. If you're cut off from your pelvis, it's hard to truly feel yourself.

Now I not only run the massage studio, but also couples' retreats aimed at improving or saving relationships and marriages. I also lead training in CORE TOUCH® Holistic Sensual Massage, a deep 10-day self-discovery experience. Many people tell me that they have a life "before and after" CORE TOUCH®. For some, it's a confirmation that they are already on the right path. For others, it inspires them to make big changes in their lives or careers.

Connecting with your body often means you're no longer willing to compromise yourself. After this course, many people change their professions because they can't stay in environments that no longer make sense to them. Many work for companies solely for the paycheck but lack any deeper meaning in what they do. As human beings, we crave meaningful work and the desire to contribute to something greater than ourselves. All of this happens by connecting with our bodies and hearts, letting go of tension and blockages, and releasing long-held emotions so we show up as ourselves in a more profound and powerful way.

That's why I am so passionate about it. It definitely changed my life from being a lost Charles University student with good grades, several languages, and a nice career opening up in front of me in international politics. I felt so depressed when I imagined myself in the kind of profession that would be a natural outcome of my education. I wanted to do something meaningful, to help other people be happy, and I wanted to be happy myself. I would have died in a profession just working for money or simply fulfilling some duties. It's sad that many people have worked for decades in traditional professions without any personal fulfillment.

It's also a jump into the unknown to be unemployed, lacking security and status, or a good position on their career ladder. Because now, who are you? Do you have any values? But even those experiences are a beautiful opportunity to discover yourself. And even though there may be a window of time where you just don't know what to do, maybe you need months or even years of just looking around and searching.

What could be the next thing for you to feel satisfied, not only earning money but also feeling stimulated, inspired, and satisfied, knowing you are creating something meaningful? It's perfectly fine to have periods of time trying to find your own thing. And I can tell you, the more you are connected with your body and heart, the easier this will be for you because you can't just think about it. You need to feel it, and you need to embody it.

Basically, the work I have described and offered to others is the path to being the whole YOU. It is being aware of key questions: "Who am I? What are my talents? What are my passions? How do I want to live? What does it mean for me to live a joyful and meaningful life?" And also to realize you don't want to live anything less. And it's totally there for you.

You don't need to suppress yourself. You don't need to put on masks. You don't need to burn out in a professional position that doesn't speak to you. You can totally live a life of meaning and joy, even professionally.

This is really a body-centered experience. It's not something we can just think about—we need to feel it, we need to embody it. The more grounded we are in our bodies, the more connected we become to our hearts, our sexuality, our inner power, creativity, and self-esteem. For myself and others in this field, when we are in tune with our bodies, we start to recognize boundaries, thinking: "Oh, I have a boundary here." It becomes important to honor and communicate those boundaries clearly.

Many people, especially women, are often held back by thoughts like, "I'm not going to express my boundary because I don't want to hurt anyone." Or, "I'm not even sure if I like it or not... Maybe it's good for me…" This suppression impacts their ability to fully connect with their own body, touch, or sexuality. However, when we begin to honor and express our needs in these areas, it transforms all aspects of our lives. We gain higher self-esteem, greater self-awareness, and a deeper sense of self-love. As a result, expressing ourselves and creating becomes easier, free from the burden of self-doubt.

I believe professional fulfillment really starts with finding ways to be fulfilled on a personal level, to be happy and feel good in your own body and your life. How to be your own best friend, how to be appreciative and loving toward yourself? How to be your number one fan? Do you cheer yourself on when you have a good idea? Or do you doubt yourself? This is a personal journey, and there is never a moment when we are fully ready. It's an ongoing journey. We just keep growing.

People tend to think of sexuality or sensuality as something relegated to your bedroom. But it's our number one life force. It's the creative force. It's connected to our power and manifestation. We need to be healthy and happy, and we need to connect our sexuality with our heart. Of course, there is also the potential of a spiritual dimension, opening up to something greater than yourself. It's just the catalyst for so many good things in your life.

BUILDING THE FOUNDATION

Linda Jensen

Linda Jensen
CEPA, CFF, ChFC, CLU, CLTC, CSA, CF2, LUTCF

Linda holds several certifications, including Certified Exit Planning Advisor, Certified Financial Fiduciary, Chartered Financial Consultant, and Chartered Life Underwriter.

Linda has been sharing her knowledge through financial seminars, educating the public and business owners on a wide range of topics since 1997. She takes pleasure in enlightening clients about all facets of planning, with a special focus on tax planning. Linda's approach is to present her clients with options, enabling them to make informed decisions based on facts. She is passionate about helping her clients achieve their goals and dreams.

Contact: linda@heartfinancialgroup.com

Embracing Independence: The Self Employment Journey

By Linda Jensen

"The pearls weren't really white; they were a warm oyster beige, with little knots in between so if they broke, you only lost one. I wished my life could be like that, knotted up so that even if something broke, the whole thing wouldn't come apart." —Janet Fitch

I've never actually been fired from a job. In fact, I "fired" the company I was working for. It felt good, kind of like throwing confetti in the air after finishing a marathon.

A Fresh Start with Brad

My husband, Brad, and I met in college. I was a wide-eyed freshman, and he was a smooth-talking sophomore. He was a really bright guy and street smart. I had lived a very sheltered life and loved being around him because he was so much fun. We started dating and I didn't realize how much he liked me. My girlfriends told me, but I didn't believe them. Here we are decades later and he's my soulmate and best friend. The guy is madly in love with me, and I have never understood why.

Raising Island Babies

From the get-go, we knew we didn't want to stay in the Northeast. I grew up near Philadelphia, while Brad hailed from just outside New York City. Our college, tucked in Westchester, NY, was like Manhattan's hyper little cousin—life was happening fast, and we had no interest in trying to keep up with the rats racing toward…who knows what?

I had dreams of moving out West, but Brad had his eye on the Florida Keys. Spoiler alert: Brad won. And honestly, I wasn't mad about it. We bought a cozy place near Mile Marker 61, right by the Seven Mile Bridge. That little corner of paradise became our home for the next fourteen years. Every evening, Brad would come home, and I'd greet him with a gin and tonic, wearing my bathing suit—because, well, that's Florida life.

Both of our kids were born in the Keys, island babies from the start. When they were young, I'd whip the house into shape in the morning and spend the afternoons at the pool or the beach. We loved visiting a nearby dolphin show—think sea lions, fishy tricks, and all the marine magic you can imagine. We also had a local museum that became a favorite family spot.

Living in the Keys was like being in a small town—except the land was water, and our neighbors were fish. Everyone knew your name (or at least your boat). In the winter, tourists swarmed in droves, but the rest of the year was blissfully peaceful.

And the sunsets? Oh, the sunsets! Imagine brilliant oranges, pinks and purples painting the sky over a hundred miles of bridges and islands. With the Atlantic on one side and the Gulf of Mexico on the other, our boat was docked right outside. Within minutes, we'd be out on the turquoise Caribbean waters, cruising past sandy beaches and mangroves. Life was good—really good.

Brad was an electrical contractor, and I was a realtor. Business was booming. When I took my realtor's exam, the room was packed—2,000 people crammed in, including lawyers hoping to cash in on the red-hot real estate market. Things were flying high…until they weren't.

Twice, the State of Florida pulled the rug out from under us, canceling all construction permits and shutting our business down overnight. Stress hit us hard, especially Brad. Our son, who understood square roots at age three (yes, really), needed a more stable environment. Drugs were becoming a problem in the Keys, and it made me uneasy.

Today, that little math prodigy of ours is a theoretical physicist, by the way.

There was a stretch when fishing wasn't great, and some fishermen turned to running drugs from South America. Many ended up in jail. It was tough to watch—kids I knew were getting tangled up in that mess.

A New Life in the Pacific Northwest

That's when I knew it was time to move. We needed a reset button. So, more than 30 years ago, we packed up our lives and headed to the Pacific Northwest. We missed having seasons, and honestly, I was over hanging Christmas lights on the dock. Brad was sick of sweating buckets ten minutes after leaving the house. We were ready for a fresh start.

And now, one of my favorite stories: One day Brad got struck by lightning. Our son was about three or four at the time. But here's the kicker—Brad didn't tell me! We were out to dinner with friends when he casually mentioned it, like it was no big deal. My jaw hit the table. "Excuse me—when did this happen?" He shrugged and said, "I didn't tell you because you'd have made me go to the hospital." Apparently, for almost a year, he had to ask his helpers what my name was. And still—no big deal. Men. Sometimes I swear they're living on another planet. Of course, we women have our moments too…

Moving the four of us across the country wasn't easy. There were so many unknowns. We rented a house for a few months until we found a place we loved in a neighborhood with a huge play area for the kids. We moved in June, and by September, our son was starting fourth grade, and our daughter was off to kindergarten.

The kids thrived. They made friends quickly, and everything felt right. Brad, however, was burned out from his contracting days. I didn't want him to dive back into that stressful life. Instead, I nudged him to find a job. After a couple of months of studying, Brad passed the Washington State Electrical Administrators exam and became fully licensed. Soon, he landed a job as an estimator for a big company.

We fell head over heels in love with the Pacific Northwest. We're just a couple of hours from the breathtaking Oregon Coast, and a quick trip takes us to British Columbia. We live nestled between the Olympic and Cascade Mountain ranges; we enjoy mild weather—most of the snow stays where it belongs: up in the mountains. This place? It's our treasure, our home.

Finding Passion in Financial Services and Self Employment

Ever since college, I had dreamed of working in financial services, but that wasn't happening in the Keys—no training, no opportunities. But in the Northwest, that old dream started tugging at my heart again. In 1994, I asked Brad, "Do you mind if I get a job in financial services?" He didn't, so I passed the state insurance exam and landed a gig with Prudential Preferred. I was thrilled—it felt like I was in business without any of the overhead!

Of course, it wasn't all sunshine and roses. My first manager hated women. Yep, you read that right. I had to ride in the car with him while he went on and on about how much he hated women—including his own mother. Creepy, right? I tried to quietly transfer to another office, but he found out and started harassing me. At one point, he sent a cryptic message through another agent: "Back off before it's too late." Whatever that meant, I was out of there.

The financial industry was (and still is) a bit of a boys' club, with a 90% failure rate. But I was determined. After my transfer, my new manager advised me to sue Prudential. "You could collect six figures," he said. But I just shook my head. I was here to learn, not fight legal battles. Looking back, I have no regrets.

I didn't just "get" orphan accounts—I was *handed* them as part of my industry initiation and business training. I rolled up my sleeves, scheduled appointments, and introduced myself as their new agent, ready to make things happen. Before I knew it, I'd sold enough to get myself onto the board for great production. Conferences? I attended them all.

It wasn't long before the guys I worked with started noticing my success. They'd ask, "How are you doing this?" I couldn't help but throw in a bit of playful sass. "Well," I'd say with a smile, "I make appointments, meet with people, and accidents happen."

Reinventing Success

It took me a while to realize the office culture—these guys didn't hustle the way I did. They sat around, waiting for the manager to assign them cases. If they weren't waiting, they were answering calls from clients that weren't even theirs, hoping to steal a deal. Classy, right?

While at Prudential, I'd earned my Series 7 securities license and my CLU and ChFC designations—qualifications that cover insurance and financial planning. But despite all that, I felt stuck. I could only offer my clients a limited set of products, and that frustrated me to no end. I wanted to give them the world, but instead, I had a sliver of the pie. That's why I "fired" Prudential after working for them for three years.

Now, here I am, 30 years later, and I won't quit—unless I'm sick or dead, I'm sticking around because I love helping my clients too much to retire. This isn't just a job; it's a passion.

Since 1997, I've been teaching financial classes, and tax planning has become my favorite seminar topic.

A couple of years ago, my focus shifted to helping businesses. That was a huge change, but I embraced it. I wanted to help businesses become more profitable. I didn't "fire" my clients—no way. I just pivoted. This shift has been a big undertaking, with new marketing strategies and a focus on attracting business clients. Honestly, I'm loving this new path.

For the past two years, I've been knee-deep in research on tax strategies for business owners. I even launched a website: https://loweryourtaxestoday.com. It's a labor of love and a constant work in progress because I keep finding new strategies to share. Helping businesses become more profitable is incredibly rewarding—and with inflation hanging around, I believe businesses need all the help they can get.

Becoming an Amazon Bestselling Author

I became a Certified Exit Planning Advisor along the way, and let me tell you, there's a storm brewing for Baby Boomer business owners. They own 51% of small businesses, and the numbers don't look great. Only 20% of businesses sell successfully, while 50% are sold involuntarily—basically fire sales. With 80% of a business owner's wealth tied up in their company, having a solid exit strategy is crucial to maintaining their lifestyle in retirement. The reality? If they don't act, millions of businesses could disappear in the next decade.

On June 12, 2024, I had a conversation with a PR firm about this issue. I must've hit a nerve with my enthusiasm because my contact suggested, "Why don't you write a book?" The next morning, I sat down and drafted a chapter outline in 15 minutes. "I guess I'm writing a book," I thought to myself.

In just two months, the manuscript was done. I conducted nearly 20 interviews, hired a publicist, and got to work bringing this issue to the national stage. The book? It became an Amazon Best Seller in two weeks. But I'm not stopping there, I'm determined to turn it into a New York Times Bestseller.

The book is titled: *What is Your Exit Strategy? Maximize Your Mindset. Minimize the Minefields.* My goal is to get it into the hands of as many business owners as possible. If I can help businesses develop successful exit strategies, I'll have done my job. I am determined to change the stats. Much more than 20% of businesses must sell.

The book opens with a story close to my heart. It's about a local business owner whose company had been around for 53 years. She bought it from the original owner, grew it, and absolutely loved it. But after battling cancer for the fifth time, she was so exhausted that she gave away her clients and sold the building. Fifty-three years—can you believe that? It's practically legendary. But it's also a sobering reminder that half of new businesses sell involuntarily. It's usually a fire sale.

You don't have to waste your life feeling unfulfilled. We all have choices. Most of us are stuck in jobs that don't spark joy or passion. But here's the thing—if you can figure out what lights you up and take action, you can change everything. I've seen it happen. I've known business owners who sold their companies and used the proceeds to buy or start businesses they truly loved.

Embrace Change, Live Your Dream

Life's too short to spend waiting for the perfect time to make a change. Every day we have choices—some easy, others daunting—and it's these choices that shape our lives. Too often, people stay in jobs that drain their spirit, stuck in routines that feel safe but spark no joy. But joy isn't some distant prize; it's within reach when we dare to pivot and follow the paths that light us up inside.

Here's the truth: if we want change, no one else can make it happen for us. We can't wait for circumstances to align perfectly or for someone to hand us permission to dream. Change starts within—with a spark of courage, a leap of faith, and the belief that it's never too late to create the life we've imagined. It means embracing uncertainty, knowing that the unknown holds endless possibilities.

So, I challenge you: discover what lights you up. Dream boldly and take that leap, even if the path ahead is unclear. There will be risks, and there may be setbacks, but the reward is living a life that is truly yours—a life where passion and purpose meet. Let today be the beginning of your next chapter. The pen is in your hand. Write a story that makes you excited to wake up each morning. Dream big, leap far, and most of all, live fully.

Andrea Sinner

After 24 years with the global consulting firm Accenture, where she rose to executive managing director, Andrea Sinner boldly decided to leave and pursue a new path in law. Graduating from law school and passing the bar at age 50, she now brings a unique blend of consulting, technology, and legal expertise to her work. Driven by her passion for horses, Andrea authored *Newcomer to the Horse World* to guide horse lovers entering the equestrian community and serves equestrians through her estate planning firm, Stable Legacies PLLC. She also founded Equine Consigliere, a non-legal advisory firm, to help clients apply her books' insights to supporting the horses in their lives.

Contact Andrea at www.andreasinner.com

Horses, Purpose, and the Courage to Start Over

By Andrea Sinner

"Life isn't about finding yourself. Life is about creating yourself."
—George Bernard Shaw

Finding Stability: Adapting To a Tumultuous World

My childhood was a whirlwind of moves every two to four years, driven by my father's work. Each new location offered opportunities to learn and adapt, leaving me rarely feeling rooted in a community. Adding to the regular upheaval were dramatic changes—my mother's death when I was 12, my father's remarriage, and a thousand-mile move that separated me from my older brother. Amid this instability, school became the center of my world. My mind was naturally wired for traditionally structured learning environments. Academic excellence became my grounding force, providing consistent structure and objective recognition. I also built strong connections with like-minded students who excelled at pushing boundaries in both performance and play.

The educational system helped shape the way I viewed my potential. The feedback I received painted the following broad picture of my abilities: brilliant at math and science, competent but not remarkable at writing, and best for me to leave art and singing to the "naturally creative" kids. These assessments nudged me down a path that was logical but, in hindsight, limited my exploration of other interests.

Armed with that external guidance, I pursued a degree in Industrial Engineering. It was a fitting choice for someone who thrived on precision and problem-solving. That degree instilled rigor, discipline, and advanced critical thinking, strengthening my ability to navigate the world through the lens of logic and systems.

Building a Career: Thriving Through Learning and Growth

After graduating, I was left with a question many face: What does one do with all this education and training? Consulting was a natural fit for someone adept at shifting between communities, solving complex problems, and thriving on intellectual challenges. I entered the process and technology consulting world and developed my career at the global firm Accenture from 1990 to 2014. What began as a chance to apply my skills quickly became all-consuming.

Consulting was fast-paced, intellectually rigorous, and deeply fulfilling. I thrived in that environment. Traveling the world to work on high-stakes projects, navigating the intricacies of business transformations, and implementing large-scale technology solutions was exciting and demanding. The complexity of the problems we tackled made each day stimulating, continually challenging me to learn, grow, and push beyond my previous limits.

After almost a decade of living this intense professional life, I recognized the need for balance. As a child, I had always loved horses, but we never had the resources or stability to pursue that interest. With my growing income, I decided to revive that childhood passion. Wherever work took me, I found a place to take riding lessons. Horses provided an outlet beyond clients, powerpoint, and high-stakes negotiations. Rediscovering that passion grounded me, providing balance amid the demands of corporate life.

Despite the relentless pace, I couldn't help but feel grateful for finding my way to Accenture immediately after undergrad. I stumbled into a career aligned perfectly with my well-developed skills and expertise. Consulting allowed me to solve complex problems alongside some of the brightest minds committed to adding value and helping our clients succeed. It also allowed me to travel the world, fulfilling the need for movement ingrained in me from childhood. I loved the Accenture experience—limitless potential, integrity-driven work, and high-performing teams—it was a transformative time. The satisfaction of working with great clients, delivering meaningful results, and building enduring relationships was deeply rewarding.

Redefining Success: Recognizing the Need for Change

Despite my success in consulting, after two decades, a subtle contemplation began to surface. I couldn't ignore a growing question: Just because I was good at something, did that mean I should spend most of my waking hours doing it? The first clear sign came from a friend who overheard me on a high-stakes business call and later remarked, "You sounded brilliant and also like you could do it in your sleep." That offhand comment lingered, sparking deeper introspection about my trajectory.

Working in your zone of excellence—where, as Gay Hendricks describes in *The Big Leap*, you have honed your abilities over time and achieved exceptional proficiency—can create a deceptively comfortable space. You're valued for your contributions and, often, you make a good living. This comfort often makes it hard to justify a change unless a clearly superior alternative presents itself. And at that point, I had no clear alternative to pursue. I often joked about longing to be made redundant, believing that a forced career shift would ultimately be beneficial. However, redundancy isn't offered to those consistently rated at the top of their cohort. Instead, you get offered more work, responsibilities, and opportunities.

Taking a Pause: Reflecting and Reimagining

At that critical juncture, I sought the help of a life coach to sort through my conflicting narratives. Should I stay or should I go? I could articulate everything I loved about consulting—the people, the challenges, the intellectual stimulation. And yet, I could also express why I wasn't sure the path was sustainable for me, especially with the relentless travel and the demands of the 24/7 work cycle. My coach was insightful, but even she seemed stumped. She told me she could usually sense which direction a client should go, but both options seemed valid in my case.

Then she asked a simple yet profound question: "What would the world look like if you put yourself first?" I realized that most of my considerations related to staying or leaving—were externally focused. I didn't want to leave behind the people I mentored or let down the clients

I had built relationships with. That question fundamentally shifted my perspective. What would it look like if, for once, I prioritized my well-being and desires? And was I even sure what those desires might be?

The answers weren't immediately clear, but a seed was planted. Eventually, I decided to take a leave of absence—a ten-month trial run to see what life would be like without consulting. During that time, I realized that I could thrive without Accenture, and–even though I was an executive managing director–the firm could thrive without me. I knew these things intellectually, but after more than two decades at the firm, I needed to experience them emotionally.

Turning the Page: Making a Bold Career Reset

Sometime after that, one casual day while sitting on my deck with a friend, the direction of my career took a sharp turn. We were discussing issues involving self-dealing politicians and government dysfunction in our small town. During a conversation about my options, my friend remarked, "If you were a lawyer, you could help more."

My family had no lawyers, and I didn't even know any. Yet, her comment sparked something inside me. It became an "Etch A Sketch" moment, where you shake things up and start anew. After so many years in one career, the choices typically narrow to three: continue moving up, shift laterally, or boldly move out. I chose the final option: to embark on an entirely new path.

Within three weeks of that patio conversation, I had applied to law schools, registered for the LSAT, and given notice to my professional home of twenty-four years. My transition would take several months, but I had made the decision. Though I didn't have a clear plan for where this shift would take me, I never doubted my decision. Over the years, I had learned to trust my gut, even when I couldn't rationally explain my decisions. This was one of those times.

Pursuing Passion Over Logic: Returning to School

By most standards, starting law school in my mid-forties was unconventional. What made it further unique was that it defied career-path logic—it was driven by curiosity, courage, and a touch of audacity.

For the first time, I pursued something because it intrigued me, not because it fit neatly into a defined plan.

I entered law school with a confidence that most of my peers, who were half my age, didn't have. I had already built a successful career and wasn't concerned about failure. If law school didn't work out, it simply meant it wasn't the right fit. Unlike my younger classmates, who were anxious about their first professional steps, I knew I would be successful regardless of how this new endeavor turned out. And, importantly, I had already built enough financial security to test a new direction without the pressure of needing an immediate return.

Law school introduced me to a whole new world of opportunities. The skills I had honed in consulting—critical thinking, problem-solving, and strategic planning—translated well to the study of law. I also gained new skills, such as discerning relevant facts, building persuasive narratives, and arguing competing viewpoints. While studying law, I built friendships with people from a different generation, which proved both invigorating and enlightening.

With my new law degree, I found opportunities to have a broader impact. I led the American Bar Association's Commission on the Future of Legal Education, began co-teaching a law school elective on the future of legal practice, and eventually opened an estate planning law firm.

Combining Passion with Purpose: Embracing My Zone of Genius

Everyone has a "unique blend of skills, experiences, and passions," but figuring out how to integrate them meaningfully is a lifelong journey. After building a foundation in engineering, technology consulting, and executive leadership and adding legal expertise to the mix, I still felt something was missing. Despite all my achievements, I continued to ask myself: Had I truly found my purpose? And was I operating in my "Zone of Genius" (as opposed to simply my "Zone of Excellence") as Gay Hendricks described in *The Big Leap*?

For years, I had been trying to discover where joy might intersect with my unique gifts. The final piece of the puzzle came when I realized I had not yet fully embraced one of my deepest passions: horses. They had been a source of great joy, grounding, and meaning for me, yet they had remained a hobby separate from my professional life. I had spent years honing my business, technology, and law talents—but what if I could combine those with my love for horses?

Bringing together my love of horses and professional expertise unlocked entirely new opportunities. I knew I wanted to create something that would allow me to help others—people who cared deeply about their animals. And so, I launched Stable Legacies PLLC, an estate planning firm dedicated to serving the equestrian community, and other ventures requiring my problem solving, analytical, and client service skills. Now, when applying my well-honed skills, I not only work effectively but also experience a state of flow much more of the time, allowing me to add greater value.

My work at Stable Legacies focuses on helping equestrians plan for all of their loved ones, including both two-legged and four-legged family members. By creating comprehensive estate plans that consider the care of horses, I can help clients ensure their beloved animals are cared for, no matter what life throws at them. This approach combines my legal expertise with a deep understanding of the unique needs of horse owners, aligning perfectly with my talents and interests.

I had learned so much from joining the horse world later in life and realized there were many others like me—people passionate about horses, or with horse-crazy kids, who were successful in life but felt out of place because they hadn't grown up in the horse world. This inspired me to write my first book, *Newcomer to the Horse World: How to Do Right by Horses… and Not Be Taken for a Ride*. This book was my way of giving back to the equestrian community by sharing what I had learned and helping new and aspiring horse lovers navigate the sometimes complex and opaque world of horses.

Beyond my legal practice and book, I founded Equine Consigliere, a non-legal advisory firm that mentors horse owners through the decisions and challenges of caring for horses. Through this venture, I provide one-on-one advisory services, offering tailored advice on everything from choosing the right barn to managing the long-term responsibilities of horse ownership. My corporate experience enables me to effectively connect and communicate with accomplished adults needing support. Equine Consigliere allows me to work closely with people who share my values, helping them build positive relationships with horses and horse people.

Making Best Use of My Gifts: Supporting Horse People and Their Horses

We each have a unique blend of talents, experiences, and interests that, when combined, can create something powerful. It takes time to discover how those pieces fit together, and their form often evolves, but the journey is rewarding and the outcomes fulfilling. Today, I am blending my engineering, consulting, leadership, and law expertise with my passion for horses to provide valuable services to my clients that are aligned with my values.

Through my various ventures—Stable Legacies, Equine Consigliere, and my writing—I now have a broader opportunity to impact the world positively. I am leveraging all the tools I have developed over the years to help people find joy in horses and ensure their well-being. My mission is to ensure that horses are cared for properly throughout their natural lives and that their owners feel supported and informed in their responsibilities.

Decades of trial, exploration, and career shifts brought me here, and I wouldn't change a thing. Each phase of my life has contributed to the person I am today and my work. Whether it's helping a family plan for their horses' future, mentoring someone new to the horse world, or educating people through my writing and speaking, I am deeply fulfilled by how my life has evolved. And I look forward to improving how I add value to equestrians and, by proxy, their horses in the years to come.

My story is a testament to the idea that the path forward isn't always clear—but if you keep honing your skills and following your passions, you create yourself. I hope my story is instructive, or even inspiring, to anyone considering a career shift or feeling stuck in a role that no longer serves them. It's never too late to start over, rethink your journey, and integrate everything that makes you uniquely you.

The road has been filled with twists, turns, and detours, and I wouldn't have it any other way. Every opportunity, challenge, decision, career change, and life shift has drawn me closer to my purpose: supporting like-minded lifelong learners and creating a better world for horses.

With each passing day, I feel even more resolute in answering, "Yes!" to the question Clarissa Pinkola Estés so beautifully posed as the one we might be asked at the end of our days: "Did you make best use of the gifts I gave you?"

Tam Patane

Tam Patane is a seasoned brand and design professional with expertise in brand identity development and design for small businesses. Her work also includes book design and formatting, bringing a unique artistic touch to each project. Tam's diverse background spans multiple industries, including science, art, and finance, earning her a reputation for versatility and creative innovation. Lastly, Tam is deeply passionate about fitness and health. She actively gives back to the community, most notably by participating in charity bike rides, such as cycling down the California coast in just seven days to support the AidsLifecycle community.

You can reach Tam Patane at the following places:
Personal website at http://www.tampatane.com
LinkedIn at https://www.linkedin.com/in/tampatane/
or view her photography on Instagram @tamnitall

The Art of Starting Over - Murder, Suicide and Work

by Tam Patane

"Success is not final, failure is not fatal: It is the courage to continue that counts." —Winston S. Churchill

Starting out in my career felt like navigating the streets of San Francisco on a foggy morning. I had doubts about my choices—did I choose the right degree? Was I in the right place? Would I even find a job in my field? After earning my biology degree from a local university, I found myself quickly needing a job to support my post-college apartment life. With only the experience of retail sales and swimming coach, I secured temporary work at a Silicon Valley software company in the purchasing department. Before long, I was hired permanently and promoted to the unusual role of expeditor. This job involved building relationships with overseas vendors to ensure timely product shipments, often negotiating to resolve delays. It was a valuable learning experience that gave me insight into the working world.

About a year or two into my role, I was called for jury duty and was selected to serve on a case more complex than I could have imagined: a murder trial involving four defendants from a motorcycle club accused of killing a young man. Before the trial began, one defendant was murdered, reducing the case to a trial with three defendants. Who could have anticipated this? Typically, we only serve on juries for misdemeanors, traffic cases or civil lawsuits. The situation was rather disconcerting.

Fortunately, my company allowed me to be paid for the days I missed work, which were Monday through Thursday, while at work only on Fridays during the trial. The trial stretched on for three long months, a parade of bikers, convicts and very scary and scared individuals testified. Ultimately after two long weeks of deliberations the result was a conviction of the men involved. I tried my best to complete my weekly tasks in a single day, but it proved impossible without assistance. During that time, I felt immense stress and guilt over not fulfilling my work responsibilities; this was compounded by the burden of sentencing three men to life in prison and lingering fears of retribution from other motorcycle club members involved in the trial. As a result, I decided to quit my job, leave town and move to the mountains.

The cold weather and the lack of job opportunities in the small, mountain town didn't provide much of a reprieve, so after about a year I moved back home to Silicon Valley. Fortunately, I soon discovered a unique opportunity to finally use the biology degree I received in college as a clinical research associate at a small biotech company. Little did I know this was just the beginning of an intense journey through the medical device landscape.

It started easily but fast forward five years. I was heavily invested in the final phase of getting a medical device approved by the FDA, overseeing phase four clinical trials. This monumental task required every patient from previous trials to return for a final visit, totaling about 10,000 patients across more than 20 clinical sites in the U.S. During a critical meeting with the C-suite executives, board members and scientific advisors, it became clear that the short timeline of five months was, in their eyes, impossible. Despite the intimidating nature of the task, my small team of five—my manager, teammates, and I—accepted the challenge with the determination of a small hurricane.

However, the challenges surmounted quickly. The Vice President of Regulatory had left unexpectedly prior to the start of the project, leaving our clinical manager to shoulder the department's responsibilities. Unfortunately, the pressure proved too much, mental strain became a problem and she left on medical leave. One month in and with no leadership, it was decided that our team was to be led by the marketing and sales managers, who had minimal clinical experience.

To tackle our monumental task, we pulled together our resources and hired extra help in the form of clinical site managers to remotely coordinate with physicians and patients. Yet, reaching out to patients we hadn't seen in years—before the internet era—was an intimidating challenge. Our workdays stretched to 10-12 hours, often spilling into weekends. As the final month and the Fourth of July approached, we finally managed to secure visits for most of the patients. We were granted a day off for the holiday, but when we returned, something felt wrong. One of our co-managers was frantically searching for his counterpart. It turned out that he believed a temporary worker had taken his life at the job site over the weekend. Soon after, we discovered that the person who had committed suicide in the back of the lab was the co-manager we had been searching for. It was almost too much to bear as we approached the deadline for the FDA. A funeral, an extra day off and then back to work. It was not something I was prepared or wanted to do but through resilience and lack of knowing any other way, the project got completed.

Shortly after finishing the project and more than ready for some time off, I was invited to a wedding event aboard a cruise to the Bahamas. While resting, regaining some of my composure and enjoying celebrating with my friends, a strange mole on my shoulder gave me pause. A nervous visit to the doctor revealed malignant melanoma. Not being sure of the full physical ramifications but understanding that the reality was that my health may have been in jeopardy due to an immense amount of external stress, I decided that my well-being had to take precedence. I turned down a promotion as a manager and made the difficult decision to leave the company.

I recovered from cancer, but the shock lingered. Now with multiple years of work experience, I have easily transitioned to another clinical research position. Unfortunately, it was not meant to be before my first year was over, unethical practices were revealed at the highest levels of the company. My manager resigned, and very quickly thereafter, I chose to step away from the career of clinical research altogether.

After a period of soul-searching and some help from career counselors, I leveraged my research background into a different research area, finding and recruiting talent. I began at a small executive recruiting firm but quickly realized the culture wasn't a good fit, leading me to move on after a year. Eventually, I found my way into the field of human resources, where I spent nearly a decade exploring various roles. One manager saw potential in my organizational skills and encouraged me to take on planning company events. While doing events I was tasked with the design of invitations, posters and announcements. This sparked my passion for design, leading me to request financial support from the company for me to complete an online graphic design degree.

With new skills and a growing portfolio, all while working full-time as an HR Manager, I started freelancing and launched my own design business. After about three years, I applied for a Publications Director position, confident in my experience and creative vision. I was hired, marking a significant turning point in my career.

It took some time to discover my passion, and even longer to turn it into a career. I loved what I was doing, and the days went by quickly. Along the way, I worked for several companies, advancing both my career and my salary. It started as a graphic designer and then marketing and brand management. During this time, I was able to stay actively and happily engaged in the design process.

My most recent experience in the corporate world ended on a sour note, unfortunately. After spending about seven years in a job I loved and at a company I truly enjoyed, a new manager was brought in. Soon my core team began to shrink due to growth and movement to other companies. Our previously small group went from four members to three, and eventually, only two of us remained. The decision was made not to replace the departing team members, leaving the remaining workload to the two of us.

This was happening during an especially challenging time in my personal life. I was going through a divorce after a long marriage and dealing with the loss of my dad while settling his convoluted estate. On top of that, with the added pressure at work, I was once again diagnosed with cancer, malignant melanoma. After being cancer-free for so many years, stress took its toll. The emotional and mental cost of a cancer diagnosis became overwhelming, and I had to take a leave of absence.

After my medical treatment, I spent five weeks focusing on my well-being through therapy and quiet reflection. I returned to work eager to begin anew with fresh energy, only to discover that I had been laid off. It was yet another blow, adding to the multiple challenges of my divorce and the loss of a loved one.

I don't know if I will ever get used to the big waves of emotion in employment gains and losses including in this most recent pivotal moment but it led me to once again reevaluate my career. After years in the corporate world, I continuously yearn for balance and independence. I recognize that each transition has equipped me with the skills and resilience to start over once again.

Life's twists and turns have continuously shaped my journey, and I am currently focused on exploring ways to add value while crafting a fulfilling life. At present, I am utilizing my skills by offering graphic design and visual improvements to support the businesses of colleagues and friends. This allows me to apply my expertise in a meaningful way while contributing to their success. However, my journey of professional self-discovery is ongoing, and regardless of external circumstances, I am excited to see where it will lead in the future.

Rhonda Hunt

Rhonda Hunt is a dedicated Licensed Marriage and Family Therapist (LMFT), EMDR (Eye Movement Desensitization and Reprocessing) Specialist, and Certified Sedona Method Coach with a passion for helping people navigate their emotional challenges and trauma. With over two decades of experience in the mental health field, Rhonda has cultivated a deep understanding of the complexities of human psychology and relationships. As an LMFT, Rhonda specializes in working with individuals addressing issues such as communication breakdowns, conflict resolution, relationship dynamics, personal growth, and healing.

Over the last decade Rhonda has increasingly used the Sedona Method with clients. The Sedona Method incorporates the practice of "releasing," which involves energetically letting go of negative emotions and limiting beliefs.

www.RadicalGreatness.com
RGHunt@RadicalGreatness.com

Time's Gentle Hand

By Rhonda Hunt

"As you start to walk on the way, the way appears." —Rumi

I remember one morning when I discovered a cocoon in the back of a tree just as a butterfly was making a hole in its case and preparing to come out. I waited awhile, but it was too long-appearing, and I was impatient. I bent over it and breathed on it to warm it. I warmed it as quickly as I could, and the miracle began to happen before my eyes faster than life. The case opened; the butterfly started slowly crawling out, and I shall never forget my horror when I saw how its wings were folded back and crumpled; the wretched butterfly tried with its whole trembling body to unfold them. Bending over it, I tried to help it with my breath, in vain. It needed to be hatched out patiently and the unfolding of the wings should be a gradual process in the sun. Now it was too late. My breath had forced the butterfly to appear all crumpled, before its time. It struggled desperately and, a few seconds later, died in the palm of my hand. That little body is, I do believe, the greatest weight I have on my conscience. For I realize today that it is a mortal sin to violate the great laws of nature. "We should not hurry, we should not be impatient, but we should confidently obey the external rhythm." — Zorba the Greek by Nikos Kazantzakis

As I reflect on my journey in life, I resonate deeply with this poignant lesson about patience and timing. My life has often felt like a series of missteps, but each one has ultimately led me to where I am today. I am a late bloomer, transitioning from an aspiring actress to an elementary school teacher, and finally finding my true calling as a marriage and family therapist and Sedona Method coach.

In my youth, I felt adrift, a common theme that echoed throughout my early adulthood. Growing up in Los Angeles, I often flirted with the idea of becoming an actress. I enrolled in acting classes at a local community college, but despite my enthusiasm, a sense of direction eluded me. My childhood was tumultuous, leaving me grappling with a deep-seated desire for love and validation, which often clouded my aspirations.

In my early twenties, I took a job as a tour guide at Universal Studios. Surrounded by fellow aspiring actors and creatives, I thought I had found my tribe. However, the rejections that come with auditions took their toll on my self-esteem. I lacked the resilience needed to thrive in such a competitive environment. Instead, I began conversing with those who had chosen teaching as a profession, intrigued by their stories. Their passion ignited a spark in me, and I decided to pursue a career in education.

With newfound determination, I completed my associate's degree. I applied to a college known for its strong teaching program and enrolled as a Liberal Studies Major with a concentration on elementary education. I also minored in theater arts. I was the first person in my family ever to enroll in a university. This was a turning point in my life, marking my first step into a structured and purposeful path.

Upon completing my credentialing program, I stepped into the classroom as a teacher. I poured my heart into my work, loving the moments I spent with children. My desire to receive love transformed into a desire to give love, but I quickly realized the challenges of teaching were overwhelming. The demands of lesson planning, paperwork, and managing classroom behavior drained my energy and enthusiasm.

Regrettably, conditions deteriorated rather than improved. I found myself in an inner-city school, where behavioral issues proved to be particularly formidable. Transitioning from a small town to the bustling urban environment of Los Angeles, I experienced culture shock, despite my roots in the city. My time at the urban public school presented significant challenges, including a particularly alarming incident where a fifth-grade student threatened me with a pair of large scissors, staring me down as she declared her intention to stab me. In that moment, standing face-to-face with a student of comparable size, I summoned every ounce of courage and asserted, "Put those scissors down. You are not going to stab me. Put those scissors down now." Thankfully, she walked away; however, she proceeded to menace the other students in the classroom. I promptly called the office, urgently requesting assistance for a student who posed a threat to her peers. After a second call yielded no response, I escalated my plea, insisting that the police be summoned, as the situation had become dangerous. At last, my principal and two teachers rushed in, physically removing the student, who was kicking and screaming, and hurling insults as she was escorted from the room. The experience left me profoundly shaken.

In the aftermath, I wrestled with a critical question: should I continue my teaching career? Despite my doubts, I decided to give it another two years, hoping to find my footing. I transferred schools for a fresh start, but life soon presented another turning point—becoming a mother. The birth of my son shifted my priorities, leading me to reassess my future. I chose to embrace motherhood fully, stepping away from teaching. This decision, while daunting, felt right. I had given so much to my students, but now it was time to focus on my family.

With my newfound role as a mother, I also felt a call to return to academia. I pursued a master's degree in marriage and family therapy, excited about making a meaningful impact. The transition from teacher to therapist was relatively smooth, yet the demands of earning my licensure loomed large. I was to complete 3,000 hours of practicum experience and all the while my family expanded with the birth of my daughter. I was torn between dividing my time with my children who I wholeheartedly adored with finding the time and energy to focus on accruing the hours. The task at hand was daunting, but I managed.

After a decade in the field, I felt a disconnection from my purpose. My personal experiences and the emotional weight of being a therapist often left me feeling drained. Then, in 2008, a traumatic event sent my life spiraling. I was living in survival mode, grappling with my own PTSD, sharing my struggles with a friend who suggested I try the Sedona Method.

Initially skeptical, I delved into the Sedona Method, a self-help technique designed to help individuals release unwanted emotions, thoughts and beliefs. I immersed myself in a comprehensive 20-CD course, gradually finding clarity and healing. Through this process, I recognized that my struggles often stemmed from my desire to control outcomes, both in my life and my clients' lives. The Sedona Method offered me a way to let go of these burdens, transforming my approach to therapy. I discovered renewed passion and began to integrate the method into my practice. It was as if I had finally found the missing piece of the puzzle.

As I deepened my understanding of the Sedona Method, I attended various seminars and workshops. When the opportunity arose to train with Hale Dwoskin, I eagerly seized it. For 18 months, he became my mentor, guiding me through the intricacies of the method and expanding my perspective on emotional freedom. This period felt like the culmination of my life's journey—a sense of fulfillment I had long sought. Now a certified Sedona Method coach, my heart is full, and I am invigorated by the chance to share this transformative power with others. The method has taught me that love exists within me, waiting to be shared. I no longer seek love outside myself; instead, I live in a state of abundance, giving and receiving with no limits.

I began teaching in my mid to late twenties, feeling like a novice among seasoned educators. However, my life experiences offered unique insights that enriched my perspective. Pursuing my master's degree at 35 further distinguished me from younger classmates.

I reframed my understanding of timelines, realizing that everyone has their own path. Now, at 60, I remain open to future possibilities. I embrace the idea that life is not a race; it's a journey of self-discovery and growth. The Sedona Method has equipped me with the tools to navigate this journey with grace and confidence. Life is continuously unfolding, and I'm only just getting started.

The act of letting go, or releasing, is a powerful technique that can support individuals throughout their lives. The Sedona Method provides a tangible framework for emotional liberation, enabling people to release negative emotions, limiting beliefs, and inner resistance.

As I reflect on my journey, I recognize the beauty in the timing of life. Each challenge, each transition has shaped who I am today—a late bloomer, yes, but also someone who has discovered a profound sense of purpose and love.

Harish Rao

Harish Rao is the CEO of Seguros Muskus N.V., representing New India Assurance across Curaçao, Bonaire, and St. Maarten. He also leads Finsight Global B.V. in financial services and founded Aconter Ltd. and Partem Education LLC to support global business growth and knowledge sharing. A Chartered Accountant, Harish is deeply involved in community service through Reaching the Sky Foundation in Curaçao. Beyond work, he's a speaker, blogger, and volunteer coach, currently authoring his first book. His vision centers on empowering others to achieve their goals through education and business acumen.

Cell: (599-9) 527-7490 Email: Harish@finsight.global

You Can Make Your Choices

By Harish Rao

"If I can do it, anybody can." —Anonymous

I've worked in many organizations since completing my Chartered Accountancy in India, (equivalent to the CPA in the U.S.). Despite financial challenges, my parents always ensured that I had access to a good education. That foundation paved the way for my career.

However, despite landing good jobs, I found myself leaving each and every one of them. Why? Over time, my ego would get in the way, or I'd simply lose interest. I often felt bored or frustrated with the idea of being 'bossed around.' I wanted to be in control. In hindsight, I now realize that every time I quit, I wasn't giving up; I was preparing myself for something bigger.

Every time I faced challenges at work, I walked away instead of trying to fix the situation. But that was my way of paving the path to entrepreneurship. I started as a solopreneur, then gradually expanded by hiring employees, and today, I run several companies. Each time I quit, it wasn't because I was giving up — I was getting ready for the next step, even though I didn't always realize it.

Back then, I was arrogant and brash. I was unwilling to compromise, and that was especially true when it came to things like quality and respect. I'm still uncompromising about those values today. I've even walked away from clients who were paying me $50,000 a year for over 25 years, simply because I didn't feel valued. For me, respect and value are more important than money.

During my younger days, I would be aggressive and quick to anger. I wore my emotions on my sleeve, and my temper flared easily. I was always searching for a workplace that reflected my values — where people worked from the heart, not just for the paycheck. I wanted less bureaucracy, less paperwork. Coming from an accounting and insurance background, I hated seeing clients buried under mountains of forms and red tape.

Each time I quit a job; it wasn't just about the work conditions — it was also about how I valued myself. Sometimes I felt undervalued, and other times, maybe I overestimated my own worth. But ultimately, leaving those jobs helped prepare me for the next level. I wasn't just quitting a job; I was stepping toward becoming my own boss and, later, employing others across the globe.

When I first left India for Curacao at 30, I almost went back after two years because of how difficult things were. But by the time I was 37, I'd adjusted to island life and realized I wasn't going back. The lifestyle and work culture here are so different from Asia, Singapore, or China. Curacao has a more relaxed pace, and it's a close-knit community.

Living here has taught me to embrace a more balanced, community-oriented lifestyle. For example, my best friend lives just a minute away and my office is a 7-minute drive from home. If we feel like catching up at 5 p.m. with friends, by 9:15 we're already back home after spending quality time together. It's hard to find that kind of spontaneity elsewhere, where everything has to be planned well in advance. Here, you can truly live in the moment and experience a deep sense of community.

That sense of connection extends to my work. I prioritize respect, kindness, and maintaining strong relationships — both in business and in life. Those values drive me now, and I focus on finding balance between work, family, and community.

I've gone from being a solopreneur to becoming a serial entrepreneur, starting several companies and learning valuable lessons along the way. I've had my share of challenges — I almost went bankrupt a few times — but those setbacks taught me how to manage money wisely and invest in myself, my employees, and my surroundings.

Today, I'm a shareholder in three successful companies. I've always believed in sharing success with those around me, so everyone who works hard gets their fair share. It's that sense of community and shared purpose that has driven much of my success.

John Taylor McEntire

John Taylor McEntire is an Innovation Ecosystem Enabler and founder of Mutual Prosperity, LLC. Drawing from experiences across 40 countries and Japanese business principles, he helps tech entrepreneurs transform team alignment and scale their companies effectively. Through his Team Clarity Breakthrough program and The S.Y.N.C. Method™, McEntire guides founders beyond organizational bottlenecks to achieve their vision while maintaining work-life balance. As a certified Canfield trainer with extensive experience in global technology transfer, he bridges cultural divides to foster collaborative innovation.

Connect with John Taylor:
LinkedIn: linkedin.com/in/johntaylormcentire
Website: mutualprosperity.com
Schedule: calendly.com/johntaylormcentire

The Intuitive Maverick: Navigating Career Transitions with the S.Y.N.C. Method

By John Taylor McEntire

"The only way to do great work is to love what you do. If you haven't found it yet, keep looking. Don't settle." —Steve Jobs

Every surfer learns to read the ocean - the way waves form, how they break, when to paddle. Every alchemist learns to read omens - signs from the universe guiding them toward their personal legend. Your career journey demands both skills: the ability to read the waves of opportunity and the wisdom to follow the omens pointing toward your true calling.

I'm John Taylor McEntire, and my journey from fresh college graduate to innovation ecosystem builder has taught me that career success isn't about following a predetermined path - it's about learning to read the waves and trust the omens that guide you toward your personal legend.

The Guess Jeans Disappointment: First Lesson in Reading Waves

Picture yourself preparing to catch your first big wave. That's how I felt right before graduating college with my degree in Japanese with a business focus. The Guess Jeans opportunity to boost their Japan sales seemed like the perfect wave - one I'd been training for throughout my college years. Through multiple interview rounds, I could almost taste the salt spray of success, imagining myself riding that corporate wave between Tokyo and Los Angeles.

When I didn't get the job, it felt like wiping out on what should have been the perfect wave. Like Santiago in The Alchemist, discovering that his journey would take unexpected turns, this disappointment was actually my first lesson in reading career omens. Sometimes the wave you think is perfect isn't yours to ride - the universe has other plans for your personal legend.

First Paddle Out (TOLA, Tokyo)

Fresh from college, I landed in Tokyo as a Translation Director and Account Executive at TOLA, Inc. It was like paddling out for the first time in unfamiliar waters. My secret advantage? I've just finished reading The Alchemist by Paulo Coelho. The book's message about following omens and trusting your personal journey became my first real business strategy.

This early experience began shaping what would later become the S.Y.N.C. Method™ - a framework for navigating career transitions and fostering innovation. The method's core principles of Synchronizing with opportunities, personalizing Your approach, Naturalizing to new environments, and Communitizing through network building were taking root, though I wouldn't formalize them until years later.

In international PR, like surfing, you need to read both the obvious signals and the subtle currents. Every meeting was a wave to navigate, every cultural nuance an omen to interpret. I learned that success wasn't just about language fluency - it was about reading the unspoken messages, the cultural undercurrents that could either carry you forward or pull you under.

Learning to Read the Breaks (UMI Japan)

At UMI Japan, a boutique consulting firm, I immersed myself in the intricacies of international business. Here, I developed what I now call the "Orbs of Influence™" - understanding how different stakeholders' needs and motivations create the business equivalent of wave patterns. Each client interaction taught me the delicate dance of sales, licensing, and market entry strategies.

The Japanese bubble economy's collapse created a tsunami of change. Companies weren't just downsizing - they were fighting for survival. The economic devastation was so severe that foreign expertise became an unaffordable luxury when Japanese citizens themselves were struggling to stay employed. Like a surfer watching storm clouds gather, I could read the omens of change on the horizon.

The Critical Drop (Medical Laser Company)

Setting up the Pacific Rim division for an American medical laser company was like dropping into a steep wave during storm conditions. With Japan's economy in free fall, companies were shedding foreign staff at unprecedented rates. This intense role demanded quick adaptation and strategic thinking not just in Japan but all of Asia. I had to navigate the complexity of establishing new business relationships across multiple Asian markets. This short but crucial experience taught me about riding waves of adversity and maintaining balance in rapidly changing conditions.

Reading New Waters (Software Distribution)

Transitioning to a U.S. software distributor was like paddling out to a completely different break. The tech sector was beginning to swell with potential, though few could predict the massive waves the dot-com boom would generate. This "filler" job became a crucial observation period where I gained essential knowledge about software licensing and distribution channels. Like an alchemist studying basic elements before attempting transformation, I was gathering fundamental insights about technology commercialization that would prove invaluable in my future roles.

Mastering Hidden Currents (University of Illinois)

Joining the University of Illinois Office of Technology Management as a Technology Transfer Officer was like discovering an entirely new ocean of possibility. Here's what most people don't realize about technology transfer: it's the hidden force behind many innovations we take for granted. That smartphone in your pocket? Its touch screen, battery technology, gps, and many other of its features started as university research projects. The medications in your cabinet? Many began in university labs.

Think of technology transfer professionals as wave scouts for innovation. We study the swells of research coming out of universities, identify which ones could become powerful waves of innovation, and help guide them to shore where they can benefit society. During the dot-com boom, our office was like a favorite surf spot during perfect conditions (because of Mosaic - the first consumer browser) - tech companies were constantly paddling out, looking to catch the next big wave of innovation.

One of my most significant achievements during this period was transforming our technology export review process. The existing system was taking eight months to complete reviews - an eternity in the fast-paced tech world. By applying the beginnings of the S.Y.N.C. Method™, I managed to reduce this timeline to just one month. This involved carefully balancing researchers' eagerness to share innovations with crucial legal and export control requirements, particularly for software that could potentially have dual-use applications. The streamlined process became a model for universities and national labs across the country.

Dark Waters and Hidden Omens: The Depression Years

But even as I was helping others ride waves of innovation, I found myself caught in a dangerous undertow. Depression isn't just feeling sad - it's like being pulled under by currents you can't see, struggling to breathe while everyone on the surface thinks you're fine. On paper, I was crushing it - respected professional, prestigious institution, the whole nine yards. Inside, I was drowning.

The challenge began because my wife was battling her own demons. Like a surfer trying to rescue another while fighting the current themselves, I found myself in an impossible situation. Just when I might have become director of the office, I realized I couldn't take on more responsibility because we were a family of eight. The weight of generational struggle - remembering my mother's own battles with depression - felt like waves crashing over me repeatedly.

The Guiding Light: Discovery of Coaching

Just as Santiago found help from unexpected sources in The Alchemist, my salvation came through witnessing a colleague's transformation through professional coaching. Like finding a lighthouse in a storm, I asked my boss if I could have a coach too. This decision changed everything.

Working with that coach was like having an experienced surfer teach me to read waves in a whole new way. I started seeing patterns in my behavior, understanding my strengths more clearly, and identifying areas for growth. This experience began crystallizing the S.Y.N.C. Method™.

Riding Bigger Waves (Pacific Northwest National Laboratory)

At PNNL, I stepped into a role that demanded mastery of everything I'd learned while pushing me to expand my capabilities further. As a senior commercialization manager, I was dealing with more complex technologies, higher stakes, and broader impact. The laboratory's national security and energy research created innovations that could reshape entire industries. Each project required the precision of an alchemist and the intuition of a seasoned professional.

This period was crucial in developing my understanding of innovation ecosystems. I learned how various stakeholders - researchers, industry partners, government agencies - needed to work together to create successful innovation outcomes.

Creating New Breaks (Qatar Foundation)

Moving to Qatar Foundation as Director of IP Commercialization meant building an innovation ecosystem from the ground up in an emerging market. Qatar's market in 2013 lacked many elements we take for granted in developed innovation ecosystems: few local entrepreneurs who could commercialize advanced technologies, limited venture capital, and nascent support structures. Like an alchemist starting with raw elements, we had to create transformation from the ground up.

The Research to Start-up Program became a flagship initiative demonstrating how institutional linkages foster greater innovation. We created a knowledge transfer pipeline between international entrepreneurs and local talent, while simultaneously accelerating Qatar's startup ecosystem development. Along with creating about a dozen startups the program built lasting bridges between Qatar's research community and global markets, establishing a proven model for technology commercialization in emerging markets.

We implemented comprehensive initiatives across multiple fronts: innovative training programs equipped local researchers with commercialization skills, while our international partnership networks provided crucial support structures. Our technology evaluation frameworks helped identify promising opportunities, and we deliberately fostered connections between academia and industry. Throughout all of this, we focused on cultivating an entrepreneurial mindset within the academic community within a "win-win" construct, essential for long-term ecosystem development. Each initiative was designed to build sustainable innovation capacity that would continue growing long after my tenure.

Teaching Others to Surf (Mutual Prosperity and Nemawashi Centers)

In August 2022, I founded Mutual Prosperity, LLC, applying the fully developed S.Y.N.C. Method™ to help organizations and leaders unlock cohesive potential in their teams. Like a master surfer who now teaches others to read waves, I work with organizations to navigate complex transitions and foster innovation.

The S.Y.N.C. Method™, refined through decades of experience, helps individuals and organizations through four key principles. First, Synchronize: this means aligning actions with deeper currents of opportunity and purpose, just as a surfer syncs with wave patterns. Second, Yourself (Personalize): this involves developing your unique leadership style and strengths, like finding your perfect stance on the board. Third, Naturalize: this principle focuses on adapting to new environments while maintaining core balance, becoming one with the changing conditions. Finally, Communitize: this means building networks of mutual support and shared wisdom, creating ecosystems where everyone can catch better waves.

The Vision: Nemawashi Centers

My current vision focuses on Nemawashi Centers, inspired by the Japanese gardening term meaning "preparing the roots." Just as a skilled gardener prepares a tree for transplanting, these centers will prepare organizations and individuals for collaborative transformation.

Nemawashi Centers will be spaces specifically designed to generate optimal conditions for innovation and collaboration. These will be places where startup founders work alongside potential corporate acquirers to make the acquisition process smoother and more valuable, where educators collaborate seamlessly with policymakers to create more effective educational opportunities for their communities, and where researchers interact naturally with entrepreneurs for easier transfer and transition. They will be spaces where different worlds collide to create new possibilities across the globe.

The centers represent the culmination of everything I've learned about fostering innovation and transformation - from my early days reading cultural currents in Japan, through the technical complexities of university tech transfer, to building innovation ecosystems in challenging environments.

Riding Your Own Waves

Your career journey, like mine, will have its own unique waves to ride and omens to follow. The S.Y.N.C. Method™ isn't a rigid formula - it's a way of reading the waters and trusting your journey. Sometimes the wave you think you want isn't the one you're meant to ride. Sometimes the wipeouts lead to the most important lessons.

Remember: every surfer starts by paddling out, every alchemist begins with basic elements, and every career journey starts with a single step. Trust the process, read the signs, and stay open to where the currents might take you. Your personal legend awaits.

FROM FEAR TO POWER

Gwen Medved

Gwen Medved is a best-selling author, entrepreneur, and advocate for women and children, known for her deep commitment to family and impactful storytelling.

Gwen has been featured in Forbes, USA Today, Women's Health, and Entrepreneur magazine, and has appeared on ABC, NBC, CBS, and FOX affiliates nationwide, as well as Yahoo! News, CNBC, and MSNBC.

A member of The National Academy of Best-Selling Authors, Gwen is a recipient of both the EXPY and Quilly awards. She is the executive producer of the Telly Award-winning film *It's Happening Right Here*, which raises awareness about child sex trafficking in the US.

Gwen holds a BA from Purdue University and an M.Ed in counseling and human services from DePaul University. She is a certified Canfield Transformational Trainer and Values-Based Leadership Coach.

You can connect with Gwen on Instagram @gwenmedved or at gwenmedved.com

I Quit—The Power of Letting Go

By Gwen Medved

"Sometimes, to move forward, you have to let go of the past. Letting go of what no longer serves you clears space for new opportunities, new growth, and new success." —Jack Canfield

My boss called me into her office one afternoon. Her face was set in that stern way bosses do when they want you to feel small before they've even said a word. It was my first job after graduating from college, and on my lunch breaks, I'd been sneaking out for interviews. The look on her face told me I had been caught.

"You're fired," she said bluntly from the other side of her big fancy mahogany desk.

I felt shattered and ashamed and super afraid. Yes I had been looking for another job, but leaving by choice felt a lot different than getting canned. It wasn't just the job; it felt like I had gotten caught doing something bad and I was being punished. Like I'd actually betrayed this woman for daring to want something better. I remember thinking, *Maybe it's wrong what I have done and I don't have the right to want more. Maybe this "punishment" is what I deserve.* But that wasn't the part that stuck with me. It was when she said, "Someday, Gwen, when you run your own company, you'll understand."

I was 22 at the time, and those words made no sense to me then as I sat there feeling like a piece of shit. But she was right. Someday I would run my own company and I did have to fire people, and it sucked. That happened and the truth is, it was much harder for me to be the boss and fire someone than it was to be fired at 22. But in that young moment—getting fired—was just the start of my life trajectory and learning something much bigger, something I couldn't yet see. Getting fired because they caught me looking for another job wasn't failure; it was my next big step on my path to get where I was going. It took years, but looking back now, I see clearly that was the moment I began to understand that walking away from something not meant for me wasn't wrong—it was mandatory for my personal development and overall success and well-being in life.

Quitting Isn't the End—It's a Beginning

I grew up, in Alaska, with the kind of grit you only get from surviving a chaotic home in the wild and non traditional. As a kid, I knew I wanted more—more than the constant uncertainty, more than the brokenness that felt like it was etched into the walls of my childhood. By the time I was nine, I was hustling. My best friend and I would call up the neighbors, offering to wash their cars for five bucks, and motorcycles for less. We'd spend a Saturday going from job to job scrubbing cars and motorcycles, and walk away with $80 in our pockets. That feeling—figuring out how to make money, was my early entrepreneurialism—and it was intoxicating. It lit a fire in me.

That drive and work ethic carried me through high school, and college, through setbacks, and through moments when I thought life would crush me. But then life shifted and a new adventure began . I met a guy, fell in love, got married and built a family and it all happened in 2 fast years. My go-getter spirit from childhood got swapped out by my longing for that white-picket-fence life I never had in Alaska that I could see with my midwestern man. I got lost in the fantasy of what we could build together and it took almost thirty years to find my way back.

We started with nothing but dreams. Together, my beautiful boyfriend and I got married and became parents. We were young entrepreneurs, throwing ourselves into all sorts of possibilities and that was fast too. Everything from fishing lures and finger massagers, to exercise equipment and weight loss products. This evolved into real estate and a media company, a manufacturing company… and television stations! You name it, we invested in it. Almost immediately we gave up living in the city we loved and moved to a rural town in Wisconsin. All for the dream and to pursue the shared goal. The goal was always: build a life, make money, create security, build a white picket fence for our family. That was my goal. The possibilities were endless if we were doing it together. I loved the adventure of building this life with my love and took the hardships and challenges as a testimony to our love. My dream wasn't just about success on paper—it was about creating a home. Building a marriage and a family life based on love and where we felt safe financially. A life where we had everything. An abundance of love, and where I could be present with my kids. I didn't want someone else raising my children. I wanted to be there for them. I wanted it all and carved out pieces of myself to make the dream happen.

And for a while, I thought we had it all. We built our legacy. Together. I was the CEO of our family, he was the CEO at work. He worked hard. I worked hard. We worked hard. We divided and conquered for our success. The work ethic was formidable. We were building a life, one I thought we both wanted. But over time, it began to feel like we were building separate lives. He was chasing success out in the world, while I was holding it down at home, and the polarity became extreme. What started out as a great adventure together and felt romantic and passionate, became separate and lonely, chaotic and intense. On the outside, we looked like a strong family, but on the inside, I was overwhelmed, sad, frustrated and lonely. My kids could feel the undercurrents of tension more often than not. The love and partnership I offered and wanted—felt further away with every deal, every success, every dollar. We had worked so hard to achieve so much and now that we had it, I lost what mattered most to me.

Staying for the Sake of Family

I wasn't ready to quit, because I thought our love was strong enough to endure and repair so I stayed. For a long time, I wanted to believe it would all work out. I stayed because I loved my husband. I stayed because I adored my family. I stayed because I was deeply attached to the potential I saw in our relationship. I became an expert at avoiding the truth, convincing myself that if I just held on a little longer, everything would fall into place. I future-tripped—telling myself that once the chaos subsided, once the next crisis was behind us, we'd finally come together, and all the hard work, sacrifice, and effort would pay off. I was chasing the dream of building a life we could both be proud of—the long standing white picket fence I built my hope around. Sometimes it felt that way, and then it wouldn't. The ups and downs. I thought that was how a strong marriage was built on the good and bad times. I wanted to be married forever. But deep down, my intuition was screaming and it only got louder and louder. I felt the cracks widening—the dishonesty, the disconnect from the values that once anchored us: love, loyalty, honesty. Family. I wasn't ready to face it yet, but slowly, I began to realize that no matter how hard I tried, this life wasn't the one I had imagined. It was slipping through my fingers, and I could no longer ignore it.

I kept telling myself that we were in it together. I was not ready to quit. I did not want to let go. I was so deeply invested in the life we were building that I refused to acknowledge the cracks beneath the surface. While I poured everything into my marriage and family, and the hope of it all, I was living that vision alone. Delusion is believing the illusion. I convinced myself that if I just held on a little longer, things would change—that we would somehow find our way back to each other. But the more we gained externally—the houses, the investments, the businesses—the more I lost and the more alone I became. The more separate we became. Not just from each other, but me from myself. I didn't realize it then, but I was slowly sacrificing the core of who I was just to keep the illusion alive. I was living a false version of success, because it was not based on truth and connection, honesty or love, and the toll it took was devastating. I felt like a stranger in my own life, and worse, like a failure for not being able to make it all work. The cost of holding on wasn't just the dream—it was myself. The truth was, I was terrified to leave.

The Courage to Quit—The Power of Letting Go

Walking away from—the shallow falseness of my marriage—was the bravest and most terrifying and heartbreaking thing I've ever done. I was so afraid of what it would do to my girls, and what I would be without the safety of my white picket fence and white lies marriage. Who was I if I was not the We, that we had built together? It took walking away, facing the fear and doing it anyway to come to the conclusion I had built a life carefully wrapped around mostly someone else's dreams and goals, at the expense of giving up my own. I had adopted someone else's definition of success while sacrificing my own by telling myself it was enough to make them mine too. I had spent years playing the role of partner and wife, putting myself on the back burner, compromising core values while waiting for a future happiness built on love, honesty and integrity that never came.

Quitting wasn't just about walking away. For me, it was about facing the truth. I had quietly quit myself for years in order to make things work at home and that reckoning was painfully brutal. I had spent so long chasing a white picket fence fantasy I let go of honoring myself in my own life and forgot who I was to begin with. I was not a woman born to sit quietly on the sidelines so when and why had I decided to live that way?

I understand why it was easy to live under the illusion that success is about money or material accomplishments. I had to work hard for everything, every dollar, starting early and that value got baked into my DNA. I put myself through college by saving and working three jobs. But what is all that eventual prosperity really bringing if you compromise yourself to the point you no longer recognize who you are and are miserable in your own skin? Yes, I still believe in prosperity and abundance, but not if it comes at the cost of my truth, my integrity, or my ability to be connected to those who I love deeply and those who can love me deeply in return. Letting go wasn't just about walking away from my marriage; it was about reclaiming my right to create my own definition of success, on my own terms. Today, I am learning to refocus on what truly matters to me: reconnecting with myself, cultivating deep, honest relationships, cherishing time with my girls, building out life plans and daily routines anchored in my own core beliefs. and investigating the creation of a career that feels immersive, purposeful, and joyful—like play fueled with passion. To fully step into this new version of success, I have had to release everything that didn't align with it. In the process, I have unearthed parts of myself I had buried beneath years of compromise and neglect. It wasn't just about leaving—it was about coming home. The real journey has been about rediscovering the woman I am now at my core and finally giving her the freedom to live a life that honors who I am, one that allows me to truly feel myself.

Quitting Is Play; Not Work

These days, I get to live a life that feels deeply fulfilling in the best way. I have chosen to collaborate with people, brands, and companies that are dedicated to making a real impact in the world. This is what brings me joy. I am building a life where my work feels like play—whether it's producing documentaries on critical issues like human trafficking, bringing a Broadway show to life, or helping new authors and thought leaders shape their brands. I approach everything from a place of purpose and love, building connection and creating awareness collaboratively. And the best part? I get to do it alongside my family. That's something I'll never walk away from.

But I didn't get here by holding on. I got here by letting go.

The Power of Letting Go

Choosing to walk away, quit or let go of anything or anyone is never easy, especially when you've built your identity around someone or something—a job, a relationship, or even an idea of yourself. Which is what I did in spades. I was young and in love and I had big dreams, and knew what I wanted at the time. I regret absolutely nothing. My journey is what has brought me here today! But letting go of what no longer serves you allows you to continue evolving and growing and is how you create space for the next evolution of your life. The only constant in life is change and when we cling too tightly to what we have outgrown, it gets hard to breathe sometimes, and for sure keeps you from living your best life or reaching your highest potential. Have faith that what's meant for you will find you. When you let go, you open yourself up to a world of possibility—a world that's more aligned with who you truly are.

The Courage to Know When It's Quitting Time

If you're wondering whether it's time to quit something in your life,

Ask yourself:

- Does staying in this situation/with this person energize or drain you?
- Are you living your values or compromising them?
- Are you growing, or are you shrinking in this relationship, job, or mindset?
- Are you staying because you're afraid of what happens if you leave?
- What would your nine year old self think of the life you're living today?

Quitting to Play Full Out

The choices you make will change the trajectory of your life! Today, I live a life that feels more like play. I have the opportunity to collaborate with people dedicated to creating a positive impact with their work, and also with my family, building brands that align with our values. Your time is valuable and you only have so much of it. There is an abundance of time that comes when you commit to doing what you truly love and quit the rest. After raising my daughters, I now have the privilege of helping them build their own businesses, like a healthy tinted sunscreen line inspired by one daughter's journey with PCOS. Collaborating with family is the ultimate expression of my values, and it's something I will never walk away from and will always wholeheartedly embrace.

Here's what I know for sure: We're taught to push through, to hold on because that's what success is supposed to look like. But sometimes, the most courageous and successful thing you can do is quit—quit living a life that no longer reflects your truth. If you feel that pull inside, that quiet knowing that you're ready for something more, trust it. The moment you let go, you make room for something far greater, something that aligns with who you are and what you're truly meant for.

If my journey resonates with you, and you're standing at your own crossroads, I want you to know you're not alone. I encourage you to step into your truth. Embrace the journey and possibility of creating a life, a business, or personal brand that reflects the real you. Take the first step and trust in the power that lies within you. You have everything you need—strength, wisdom, resilience—to create a life that not only reflects your deepest truth but exceeds your wildest expectations. Every ending is a gateway to a new beginning, and the future ahead is richer, fuller, and more extraordinary than you can possibly imagine right now. You are capable of transforming your life into something remarkable. So step boldly into the unknown, let go of what no longer serves you, and watch as the universe rises to meet you in ways beyond your dreams. The life you've been waiting for is ready and waiting for you—claim it.

Vickie Menendez

Vickie Menendez is a wellness guide and transformational coach with over 35 years in self-care, wellness, and holistic healing. Her journey through loss began with a stillbirth in 1980, followed by the loss of her son in 2017, her father in 2018, and, most recently, two of her children just 12 days apart. These experiences led Vickie to combine new healing tools with her lifelong wellness practices, transforming her pain into purpose. Today, she offers programs to help women, especially mothers, embrace self-care and gain tools to process any emotion, guiding them to resilience and new beginnings. It all matters.

How to work with me: vickiemenendez.com
You can find my memoir: www.motherofallmemoirs.com

The Courage to Begin Again and Again: A Story of Transformation and Finding the Strength Within

By Vickie Menendez

It takes strength to make your way through grief, to grab hold of life and let it pull you forward." —Patti Davis

My journey has been filled with moments of growth and transformation, often sparked by the most unexpected circumstances. Looking back, I see how life has a way of pushing us toward what we are meant to do, even when the path seems difficult or unclear.

I began my professional life with a passion for hairdressing, but as I progressed in my training, I discovered my true love was skincare. That shift in focus led me to a prestigious spa where I worked for several years, pouring my heart into the job, dreaming of one day having my own spa, though, at the time, I believed it was improbable. Like many in my field, I wanted a space that was mine—a reflection of my vision and my essence.

But life, as it often does, threw a curveball. When my employer found out about my aspirations, she let me go. I was devastated. I had three young children depending on me, and losing my job felt like the rug had been pulled out from under us. It was a moment where I had to decide whether to find another job or finally pursue what I had long dreamed of—opening a spa of my own.

Sitting alone late one night, wondering how I'd move forward, I found myself tuning into a Tony Robbins infomercial. His words pierced through the quiet, speaking directly to my fears and doubts. He said, "Your limitations aren't holding you back—your fear of breaking through them is." Those words hit me like a wave. It was the wake-up call I didn't know I needed, reminding me that fear had been the only barrier between me and my dreams. The comfort in my job and the regular paycheck made me think, maybe someday, but reality set in once my job was no longer my excuse for waiting. Now it was up to me. For the next 30 days, I immersed myself in his teachings, turning every lesson into an action step. It felt like I was building a bridge, one thought, one choice at a time, toward the life I had envisioned.

Tony's message brought me back to a memory from my teenage years, the day when my father and I built a rock wall together. It was hard work, and the stones seemed endless, but we kept going, one rock at a time. My dad wasn't one to hand out compliments easily, so what he said that day has stayed with me my entire life. As we placed one of the last rocks into the wall, he turned to me and said, "Vickie, I think you could do anything you set your mind to."

Those words were a rare and precious gift. My father didn't hand out compliments unless they came from his heart. Those spoken words stayed with me, becoming a source of strength that I still lean on whenever I feel fear or doubt. That wall was more than just a project—it was a testament to persistence, patience, and belief in myself. It became a metaphor for life, teaching me that with effort and determination, I could do anything I was inspired to do. That night, as I listened to Tony Robbins, it brought me right back to that memory of my father. Suddenly, I realized, this was just another wall to build—one step at a time. My father's belief in me, combined with the renewed motivation from Tony Robbins, gave me the courage to move forward.

Setbacks are often just stepping stones in disguise, leading us toward something greater. When life presents me with challenges, I return to that rock wall memory, where my father's words still fuel my strength and remind me that I can accomplish anything I am inspired to do.

Sometimes, we are inspired to aim higher, but fear holds us back. It takes something—a nudge from the universe, or in my case, being fired, a late-night motivational speech, and that day with my dad—to remind me that there's more waiting on the other side of fear. Within six months, I had opened my spa, thanks to a combination of resourcefulness and community support. I borrowed $2,000, negotiated free rent and help with the buildout from my landlord, and, with the help of loyal clients, slowly built the spa of my dreams. They believed in me, not in the perfect space or lavish decor, and that is what made it so special. My clients would ask, "What did you buy this week or this month?" They felt like they were part of this beautiful tapestry that was unfolding before us—and they truly were. They were integral to the shop coming to life.

What if I had waited for everything to be perfect, to have enough money to make it all just right? Instead, I included my clients in the experience of watching something beautiful take shape. I still get teary-eyed when I think of that spa and what it meant to both me and my clients. I armed myself with the "knowing" that everything I needed would show up. The people who were meant to walk this journey with me would walk through the door exactly when I needed them—and that's exactly what happened. It was the hardest I had ever worked, but it was also fulfilling to know that I made it happen and kept it alive and thriving. It was genuine and authentic—a come-as-you-are welcoming atmosphere. My clients loved it.

I ran my spa for 10 years, but as my family grew, I decided to be more present with my youngest son Jesse from a previous marriage, and Sebastian, who I was only months away from giving birth to. My two older children were on their own by then. This time, I knew the importance of balance. I wanted to be present for him in a way I couldn't be for my older children. It was a beautiful period of growth in a different way—motherhood in its most intentional form.

But then, life changed again. When Sebastian was 3 years old, he experienced a total regression after a couple of severe reactions to a vaccination and a strong antibiotic. It was as if a fog surrounded him; conversations produced blank stares. I had never encountered anything like this before, and I found myself searching for what I could do to help him. The years I had already devoted to health and wellness provided some guidance, but there was still so much to learn. I exhausted every avenue to bring him back to us whole and healthy. I became his healer and advocate, and over time, his symptoms faded. Sebastian went on to thrive—he consistently made the honor roll in high school and was later recognized on the dean's list in college almost every semester. I felt that everything I had done to support his wellness gave him an advantage. I believe that every modality helped him to put the pieces back together. The various modalities I used slowly erased the cobwebs, giving him a much better chance in life. This is something that I wanted to share with the world and will eventually. Early detection and action are key.

However, just when I thought we had overcome that challenge, I faced the unimaginable loss of my son in 2017 and my father in 2018 which guided me to seek a coach to teach me the tools toward healing. I had no idea that in 2023 I would experience the loss of two more children only 12 days apart. Had I not sought help and learned these valuable tools combined with the 35 plus years of self-care and wellness I don't think I could have survived it. I realized that I had been cultivating tools not just for my journey but to help others through their traumas.

After my children's passing, I knew I needed to share what I had learned about healing and resilience. It became clear that my new mission was to help women—especially mothers—navigate their pain and challenges, whether it be career struggles, personal losses, or both. I began writing, creating courses, organizing retreats, and building new pathways to serving others. I wanted to show women how to say "yes" to themselves, how to nurture their dreams, and how to heal from their wounds. The wounds that hold us captive, unable to move forward.

As I reflected on my own story, I realized that the setbacks I had faced weren't just obstacles; they were opportunities. Losing my job wasn't the end—it was the beginning of a new chapter. Losing my children, though excruciating, showed me the depth of my resilience and gave me the clarity to pursue a new calling.

You may start over more than once in your life, searching for a way forward. When that happens, consider it the universe's way of nudging you to dig deeper and open your eyes a little wider. These moments often reveal our true mission, surfacing when we are ready to heed the call. There's always a path ahead, even when it's not immediately clear. Trust that it's there, waiting for you to discover it. Make sure that your inner dialog matches the frequency of what you want. You can't possibly get that raise or start that new business if you keep telling yourself; " that it will never happen for me. It is only for the lucky few". If you study the habits of the most successful people in the world, many who started with nothing, there is a common thread between them. Everything matters. What we say, what we do, what we think, and we should never lower our expectations out of fear of failure because failure should not be an option. That is when we pivot and find another way. Never give up. I have story after story of successful entrepreneurs who said that if they quit when things got hard, they wouldn't be where they are today. We all have greatness within us. Every one of us has unique gifts that sometimes are left dormant within us. It's time to wake up that sleeping lion and let it roar.

As Tony Robbins wisely said, "We do not experience life. You and I experience what we focus on and the meaning we give to it—so choose well."

My journey has taught me that sometimes, what feels like an ending is actually a doorway to something greater. It's through those cracks in the surface that the light comes in, guiding us toward our purpose. Today, my dream is to help others find their light, even in the darkest moments. Whether they are grieving, struggling with life's transitions, or just trying to find their way, I want to be that beacon of hope, reminding them that they, too, can rise again.

This new chapter of my life, this next dream career, is about giving back. It's about turning pain into purpose and creating space for others to heal, grow, and thrive. And the beautiful thing is that I feel the spirit of my children as they walk this path with me, inspiring everything that I do. This was a soul contract that we had together—their contract with me and mine with them. A beautiful tapestry that revealed the mission I had agreed to before coming into this life experience. I find gratitude, love, and joy in everything I do. These high-frequency emotions allow me to feel the presence of my lost children, who are operating at a very high level. My ability and desire to raise my awareness and frequency allows me to get a glimpse of them and feel their presence.

Remember that no matter what happens in life, there is always a path forward if we choose to be present and open our hearts and eyes to the gifts that are trying to reveal themselves to us. Get curious about what any event in your life truly means. There is always a gift on the other side waiting to be opened. Life is always happening for us, and if we can remember that, and believe that, then we have already won.

Earl Waud

Earl Waud, known as The Hindsight Mentor, empowers individuals who feel they've fallen behind on their dreams, guiding them back to a path of clarity, purpose, and fulfillment. With a proven approach that blends empathy, personal storytelling, and success frameworks, Earl helps clients reignite their ambitions, achieve holistic success, and create lasting impact. Through his books, coaching, and mastermind programs, he offers a supportive community and actionable insights for transforming dreams into reality. Earl's own journey of resilience, creativity, and dedication to lifelong growth embodies his brand's mission: no dream left behind.

Your dreams are ready and waiting!

Contact Earl at:

earl@thehindsightmentor.com

TheHindsightMentor.com
FreeGiftFromEarl.com

From Layoff to Life's Calling: How Losing My Job Led Me to My True Purpose

By Earl Waud

"What seems to us as bitter trials are often blessings in disguise." — Oscar Wilde

Embracing the Unexpected

Sometimes, life's greatest blessings come in the most unrecognizable forms. It felt like the rug had been pulled out from under me, leaving me breathless, bewildered, and standing in the wreckage of what used to be my life. That's how I felt during the Zoom call when my manager said the words I never expected to hear: "You're on the layoff list." In that instant, all the work, dedication, and accomplishments I thought would keep me secure felt meaningless. I could hear my own voice, trembling as I said, "Why me?" But here's the thing—what I learned is that there are moments, wrapped in confusion and pain, that are actually the greatest gifts we could ask for.

What if losing my job wasn't the end, but rather the beginning—the gateway to the career I was destined for, one that lights my fire every day, one that feels like my life's true calling?

I want to share my journey of turning an unexpected layoff into an opportunity to live my purpose. My story isn't just about job loss; it's about regaining the steering wheel of my life and refusing to stay complacent. Because here's the truth: the path to discovering your dream career begins the moment you stop seeing setbacks as obstacles and start recognizing them as launchpads.

A Layoff's Shock and Awakening

Imagine this: It's a regular weekday. I'm sipping my morning coffee, logged in with my team, reviewing updates. Everything seems fine. I'm comfortable. And then, without warning, my manager's voice shakes my foundation. It's a company-wide reduction. Despite the excellent reviews, despite the hours I'd put in—I was on the list.

And in that moment, I did what most of us do. I shut off my camera, muttered something about needing to leave the call, and stared at my screen in disbelief. My mind was racing: What about my family? What about my future? Panic set in.

The first thought is almost always, "Why me?" But the truth is, asking that question only holds us back. The real question—the empowering question—is "What now?" It took some time, but slowly, that question began to surface, leading me to realize that this layoff was something much deeper. It was a wake-up call—a challenge to take responsibility, to stop being complacent, and to design my life the way I had always envisioned.

It wasn't easy. There were days when I felt defeated and overwhelmed. But gradually, I began to understand that this moment of loss was actually an invitation. An invitation to create something new, something better. It was the first step toward taking back control of my life and choosing a path that aligned with who I truly was. I started to see this layoff not as a failure but as an opportunity to finally pursue my passion.

Responsibility: The Power to Transform

You know what it's like to wrestle with blame. It's easy to blame external factors—the company, the economy, the market, the pandemic. It's comfortable to think we're the victims of circumstances beyond our control. But in truth, that mindset is what keeps us imprisoned.

I remember the conversation with my friend Veni shortly after my layoff. She reminded me that I had been doing my real dream job all along—as a coach, a trainer, a writer. She said something that stayed with me: "The universe has been laying out this path for you since you were ten years old." That's when it struck me: I hadn't lost a job; I'd been given the opportunity to finally do what I'd been training for my whole life.

Responsibility—true responsibility—isn't about accepting blame for what's happened. It's about choosing how we respond. It's about taking ownership of where we are and deciding where we're going. It's the foundation upon which we build our lives. When I finally stopped asking "Why me?" and instead asked, "What am I going to do about it?" everything changed. That's the moment I stopped feeling like a victim of my circumstances and became the architect of my future.

Taking responsibility gave me my power back. It shifted the way I looked at life. I realized I had to step out of the shadows, put my work and passion out in the open, and inspire others who, like me, felt defeated by the unexpected twists of life. It meant acknowledging my own role in where I was and deciding to take action. I realized that the only person who could turn things around was me, and that realization was incredibly liberating.

The more I embraced responsibility, the more I began to see possibilities instead of obstacles. It wasn't about finding another job; it was about finding my purpose. I knew that I had to bet on myself, take the leap, and trust that the universe had bigger plans for me. And as terrifying as it was, I also knew that it was the only way to truly live.

The Blessing of Being Forced to Pivot

There's a power in the moments where life forces us to pivot. Losing my job not once, but twice from the same company was like being thrown into the deep end. Fool me once, shame on you. Fool me twice, shame on me. But there's a lesson in that second round—an opportunity to understand that sometimes we outgrow what used to fit us.

I could have stayed bitter, angry, and fearful—and maybe for a short while, I was. But there was also freedom in it. No longer tied to the comfort of a paycheck, I had the chance to do something I had always been too scared to do: bet on myself.

My friend Veni called it serendipity. She reminded me how I had always been at my happiest when I was teaching and mentoring others—whether it was helping someone find a better career path or showing a teenager that they had what it takes to succeed. That was where my passion lived. Losing my job wasn't just a layoff; it was a nudge from the universe saying, "You're ready. It's time."

When I allowed myself to see the layoff as a blessing, everything changed. I realized that staying in that job was keeping me comfortable but unfulfilled. It wasn't challenging me anymore, and it certainly wasn't lighting me up the way my true passion did. Losing that job forced me to step into the unknown, to embrace the uncertainty, and to grow in ways I never would have if I had stayed in my comfort zone.

In those moments of forced pivoting, I found myself again. I started to reconnect with what mattered to me—helping others, inspiring people to live their best lives, and making an impact that extended far beyond the corporate world. The layoff gave me the push I needed to stop playing small and start living the life I knew I was meant to live. It was scary, yes, but it was also exhilarating. And it reminded me that sometimes, the things we fear the most are the very things that will set us free.

Reframing the Setback as an Opportunity

It's amazing what happens when you change the lens through which you see a problem. You go from feeling powerless to feeling unstoppable. From seeing yourself as someone who's been let go, to seeing yourself as someone who's been set free.

Let me be honest—it wasn't an easy shift. There were sleepless nights, moments when the uncertainty felt like it would swallow me whole. But that's when I came back to the principles I'd spent my life studying: gratitude, responsibility, belief, decision making, action taking, learning, and giving back. I reminded myself of the countless individuals who had turned their pain into power, who had faced setbacks and came back stronger.

The turning point came when I understood the reward of responsibility—the real, tangible prize—is control over my life. Control over my decisions. When I took responsibility, I stopped waiting for someone to give me a job, or an opportunity, or a reason to keep going. I created those things for myself.

Reframing my layoff as an opportunity didn't happen overnight. It was a gradual process of changing my mindset, of challenging my own limiting beliefs, and of trusting that everything was happening for a reason. I began to see my layoff as the freedom I needed to finally go after what I truly wanted. It was no longer a setback; it was my launchpad.

The more I embraced this perspective, the more doors began to open. Opportunities to coach, to write, to speak—they all started to come my way. And I realized that the only thing standing between me and my dream career had been my own fear. When I let go of that fear and stepped into my power, everything changed. I wasn't just someone who had lost a job—I was someone who had found my calling.

The Calling to Something Greater

I've learned that the worst moments in our lives can lead to the most meaningful breakthroughs. I had a dream once—while I was recovering from shoulder surgery. In that dream, I visited a place called the "Bureau of Hindsight." I was told that everything I had learned needed to be shared with others. It was time to write the book that had been sitting inside me for years.

That dream led to the creation of my first book, *Hindsight: The 7 Keys to Living Your Best Life.* Writing it helped me process everything I had learned and made me realize that every twist and turn, every layoff, every lost job, every uncertain day had a purpose. It was all preparing me for something more.

This calling—to write, to coach, to inspire—wasn't just a career move. It was a deeper, soul-level shift. It was about taking all the moments that had hurt, all the setbacks, and using them to empower others. A friend of mine once told me, God will never waste your pain. Losing my job was the beginning of my true career—the career I was meant to live.

Writing that book was a cathartic experience. It allowed me to take everything I had been through and turn it into something that could help others. It was my way of giving back, of showing others that they weren't alone, and that there was hope even in the darkest of times. And as I wrote, I began to realize that this was what I was meant to do. I wasn't meant to work in a corporate job—I was meant to share my story, to inspire others, and to help people see the possibilities in their own lives.

The calling to something greater wasn't just about me. It was about the people I could help, the lives I could touch, and the difference I could make. It was about stepping into my purpose and living a life that was true to who I was. And losing my job was the catalyst that allowed me to do that. It was the push I needed to finally say yes to my dreams and to start living the life I had always imagined.

Life Happens For You, Not To You

One of the most powerful lessons I've learned, from my layoff and from my lifelong mentors, is that *life happens for you, not to you*. At first, this can feel like just another motivational phrase—something to put on a coffee mug or a poster. But it's more than that. It's a fundamental shift in how you perceive your experiences.

When you're laid off, it's natural to feel like the world is against you. But what if you flip that script? What if you start believing that every event, every disappointment, every heartbreak is a gift? It might not look like a gift at the moment—in fact, it might look like the exact opposite. But if you can find the opportunity within the crisis, you can find your true power. My mentor Niurka likes to teach us to "mine our challenges for the jewels inside."

That belief, that certainty, was what allowed me to transform from someone whose life was defined by corporate roles, to someone who took the leap, started writing, and began the journey to becoming a full-time author, coach, and trainer. I wasn't fired; I was set free to do what I love.

Believing that life happens for you, not to you, changed everything. It allowed me to see my layoff as a blessing, as the opportunity I needed to finally step into my true calling. It gave me the courage to take risks, to follow my heart, and to trust that everything was unfolding as it was meant to. And as I look back now, I can see that every challenge, every setback, and every moment of uncertainty was leading me to where I am today.

This perspective has become the foundation of how I live my life. It's allowed me to let go of fear, to embrace uncertainty, and to trust that the universe has my back. It's given me the strength to keep going, even when things get tough, and to keep believing that there is a greater purpose to everything that happens. Life isn't always easy, but it's always working for us—if we're willing to see it that way.

Writing My Own Chapter

To everyone reading this, who might be feeling lost, who might be facing the uncertainty of a job loss or a career transition—I want you to know that this could be your greatest moment. I was once where you are—feeling lost, scared, and uncertain. But I want you to know that you are not defined by the title on your business card or the job that was taken away from you. You are defined by the passion that's inside you, the vision of who you can become, and the determination to make that vision real.

Take a step back. Reflect. Ask yourself what you really want. Maybe this setback is exactly what you needed to get out of a role that wasn't right for you, and into something that fills your heart and soul with purpose. Take responsibility, believe in your ability to rise, and recognize that losing your job might be life's way of pointing you toward something greater.

This is your chance to write the next chapter of your story. Make it a good one. It's time to lose what isn't serving you, and to find the career—the life—that was always meant for you. You have the power to create the life you want, to follow your passion, and to live your purpose. Don't let fear hold you back. Take the leap, trust in yourself, and know that the best is yet to come.

Rise, Reflect, and Realign

This journey isn't easy, but it is worth it. If you're ready to stop seeing yourself as the victim of a layoff and start seeing yourself as the hero of your own story, take the next step. Reflect, realign, and rise. There's a dream career out there, and it has your name on it. It's time to take control, to bet on yourself, and to start living the life you were always meant to live. Your next chapter starts now—make it one you're proud of.

Julie Kelly

Julie Kelly, a seasoned litigation paralegal with over 30 years in family law, is renowned for her empathy and dedication to guiding clients through challenging legal battles. A graduate of the University of San Diego's paralegal program, Julie's journey is deeply shaped by her personal experience as a survivor of a 20-year domestic violence legal battle. A certified Success Principles trainer, she's passionate about helping others reclaim their power and find purpose. Julie now shares her story in a collaborative book, offering hope and guidance.

Learn more or schedule a call at www.JulieKelly.org.

A Blessing in Disguise: Embracing the Call to Greater Purpose

By Julie Kelly

"You must be the change you wish to see in the world" —Gandhi.

The Turning Point: Embracing Life's Unexpected Shifts

There's a point in every person's life when the rug gets pulled out from under them. It might feel like the end, but for me, it was the beginning of something greater. Losing a job—a seemingly insurmountable blow—can often be the moment of clarity that wakes us up to a higher calling.

For me, being fired not once, but multiple times, opened my eyes to a path I didn't expect but one that led me to my true purpose. It wasn't easy to see it that way at first. I remember feeling like I had hit rock bottom, and it took everything I had to keep going. The anxiety was overwhelming, and I questioned my worth, my abilities, and my future. But looking back now, I realize those moments were crucial. They forced me to confront my fears, challenge my limiting beliefs, and step into a version of myself that I hadn't yet met. That's the beauty of life's unexpected turns—they push us to evolve, to grow, and to become who we're truly meant to be. It was through these challenges that I learned the importance of resilience, the strength of the human spirit, and the incredible potential that lies within each of us when we dare to dream beyond our current circumstances.

The Fear of Losing Everything

It's often said that change happens when the pain of staying the same outweighs the fear of stepping into the unknown. When I was first asked to resign from my job at the airline, I felt the ground shift beneath my feet. After three years of pouring my heart into my role, I faced a meeting where the decision was made—my time was up. The fear I felt was immediate. How would I take care of my children as a single mom? What would come next? I remember going home that day, my thoughts a tangled mess of worry and despair. The questions were endless, and the uncertainty felt like it was crushing me. I thought of all the bills that needed to be paid, the groceries I had to buy, and the needs of my children that were now my sole responsibility. But here's what I didn't know at that moment: Sometimes the universe clears out our lives to make space for something better. Losing that job was terrifying, but it also gave me the opportunity to take a step back, to breathe, and to look at my life from a different perspective. I realized that I had been settling—not just in my career, but in my belief in myself. The fear was still there, but I started to see it differently. It became the catalyst for change, the push I needed to redefine what I wanted my life to be. And with every small step forward, I began to rebuild—not just my career, but my sense of self-worth and my belief that I was capable of so much more.

From Loss to Breakthrough: The Next Step Up

Within just weeks of losing my airline job, I was hired by BP America **in** a role that not only paid significantly more but also provided me with something equally valuable: respect and understanding. My new boss treated me with compassion, allowing me the time I needed to care for my children and navigate my personal struggles. This wasn't just another job; it was an environment that supported my growth, both personally and professionally. I was able to learn new skills, take on challenges that excited me, and contribute in a way that made me feel truly valued. In this new chapter, I was given the chance to make a real impact. I was put in charge of a complex project that took two years to complete, but my efforts resulted in BP adopting my work as the standard operating procedure across the company. It was a moment of validation. I wasn't just filling a role—I was making a difference. I was thriving in an environment that recognized my potential and encouraged me to reach for more. Losing my previous job led me to an opportunity that allowed me to use my skills in a more meaningful way and build lifelong connections. This experience taught me an important lesson: **W**hat seems like a setback is often a setup for a comeback. Sometimes, the path to your dream isn't a straight line—it's a winding road filled with unexpected turns, twists that lead us to places we never imagined, but ultimately bring us closer to where we're meant to be. It made me realize that life has a way of redirecting us, even when we don't understand why at the moment.

A Calling to Help Others

It wasn't just corporate success that I found. After losing my job, I started talking to others, sharing my experiences, and, by chance, found myself helping a family in desperate need. A mother had been shot, left in a coma, and wrongfully accused. With my paralegal background, I found myself diving into criminal law—something I knew "just enough to be dangerous" about, as I'd say with a smile. I never imagined that I'd end up involved in something so serious, but there I was, collecting testimonies, interviewing witnesses, and piecing together the evidence that others had overlooked. I fought for that family for years. I helped get the case reopened, gathered testimonies, and collaborated with investigators until justice was served. The abusive man went to prison, and a woman who had almost lost her life found a voice through my dedication. This chapter of my life showed me that my true calling wasn't in paperwork or boardrooms—it was in helping people when no one else would. It made me realize that the work I was meant to do was about more than earning a paycheck. It was about using my skills, my tenacity, and my compassion to make a real difference in people's lives. I found a sense of fulfillment that no corporate job had ever given me—a feeling that I was truly contributing to the betterment of someone else's life. It was during this time that my passion for justice ignited.

Turning Pain into Purpose

My journey took me through another difficult loss when BP pulled out of my area. But each time life tried to push me down, I rose higher. I wanted to work for the district attorney's office, but the timing wasn't right. Instead, I found myself back in litigation and family law, yet always drawn to make a greater difference. I knew that helping others was my purpose, and I wouldn't stop until I found the right way to fulfill it. It was a realization that changed the course of my life forever, and I knew I was on the path I was meant to walk.

When the district attorney's office eventually did offer me a role, I stepped into the job with hope. However, the culture there was toxic, filled with complacency and lacking integrity. I knew I couldn't stay somewhere that didn't align with my values, so I left—a mutual parting that was both painful and freeing. Walking away from a stable job again felt like a failure, but deep down, I knew it was the right choice. I refused to settle. I wouldn't sacrifice my integrity just for the comfort of a paycheck. Instead, I began searching for something deeper—something that aligned with who I truly was and what I wanted to bring to the world. It was during this search that I stumbled across Marci Shimoff and Jack Canfield. I attended Canfield's "Breakthrough to Success" event, and for the first time in a long time, I felt like I was home. I described the feeling as "God bumps"—an overwhelming sense that I was exactly where I was supposed to be. For years, I had been living a life of reaction, but it was here that I realized I could live with intention. The teachings of Jack Canfield resonated deeply, and I found myself drawn to his Success Principles. It felt like everything was finally coming together, that all the struggles and setbacks had led me to this exact point, where I could transform my pain into purpose and use my experiences to inspire others. It wasn't just about surviving anymore—it was about thriving, about using every experience, both good and bad, as a stepping stone to help others and create lasting change in the world.

The Power of Choice: E + R = O

One of the most profound lessons I learned was the formula E + R = O: Event + Response = Outcome. In every situation, we can't control the event, but we have full power over our response, which ultimately determines the outcome. I had lived this truth without ever knowing its name. For decades, I had been reacting to the chaos around me—responding in fear, running for safety, feeling overwhelmed. But there came a day when I decided to change my "R"—my response.

The pivotal moment came over something as simple as orange juice. After years of enduring psychological and emotional abuse from my now ex-husband, a confrontation over an empty container of juice was the straw that broke the camel's back. It was then that I stood up, not in fear but in anger, and realized I had the power to change my life. That moment was the start of my transformation. I chose to leave, made a plan, and executed it with the precision of someone fighting for **her** life— because I was. I moved my belongings one trash bag at a time, building my escape until, finally, my children and I were free. It wasn't just about leaving my abuser; it was about reclaiming my power, changing my response, and ultimately altering the outcome of my life. It taught me that I was stronger than I had ever realized, and that the power to change my life was always within me—it just needed the right moment to be unleashed. It's incredible how one small choice can completely change the direction of your life. That day, I chose myself and my children, and it was the most powerful decision I had ever made.

Finding Strength Through Community

My journey to recovery was not without challenges. The aftermath of leaving my marriage was a legal battle that stretched on for years—draining my finances, my energy, and my patience. Yet, through it all, I found solace in the community. I attended training, connected with mentors like Patty Aubery, and became part of a supportive network that helped me see that my story wasn't just one of survival—it was one of triumph. It was the people I met during this time that lifted me up when

I needed it the most. At a Canfield training event, Patty Aubery helped me realize that I had been living the Success Principles all along. Despite the trauma and the challenges, I had taken action, believed in myself, and refused to be a victim of my circumstances. I had changed my "R" in countless situations, creating outcomes that ultimately led me to freedom and fulfillment. These people became my extended family—their encouragement and support were like a lifeline during some of the darkest moments. They reminded me that my journey mattered, that my experiences had value, and that I was capable of making a difference. It was through this community that I truly found my strength. They celebrated my victories, supported me through setbacks, and reminded me of the power of resilience. I learned that no one has to face their challenges alone; the right people can lift you higher and help you see the possibilities that lie beyond the pain.

From Victim to Victor

My story is one of moving from victim to victor. My experiences have shaped me into a person who not only understands suffering but also knows how to overcome it. I have taken my pain and transformed it into my purpose—helping others who are facing seemingly insurmountable obstacles in their own lives. It's easy to let the world define us by our struggles, but I chose to define myself by my strength. After years of litigation, personal struggle, and triumph, I have now built a coaching program that integrates my background in law with the Success Principles I learned from Jack Canfield. My mission is to help others, particularly those going through family law disputes and trauma, to navigate their journeys with integrity and strength. I want to be the guide that I needed during my darkest times—the person who stands beside you and reminds you that you are stronger than your circumstances. I often say, "Integrity wins, and love wins." At my daughter's wedding, years after the dust of litigation had settled, I found myself face-to-face with my past. My ex-husband, the man who had tried to break me, was there, but so was I—standing tall, surrounded by my children, and living a life filled with love and purpose. That moment, filled with joy and forgiveness, was the culmination of decades of resilience. It was proof that no matter what we go through, we have the power to rise, to heal, and to create a life that we are proud of. I looked at my children, my family, and realized that the life I had built was one of beauty, strength, and unconditional love. I was no longer defined by what had happened to me—I was defined by what I had overcome.

Your Setback Is a Setup for a Comeback

If there's one thing to take away from my story, it's that life's setbacks are often setups for comebacks. Losing a job, a relationship, or any stability can feel like the end, but it is often the universe's way of pointing us in a new direction—toward something greater, more aligned with our true calling. I know how hard it is when you're in the thick of it—when everything feels like it's falling apart and you can't see a way forward. But I promise you, there is a way. For those who have lost a job or are questioning their current path, know that this could be your blessing in disguise. It's an invitation to step into your power, to change your "R" in the face of life's inevitable "E," and to create the "O" that you deserve. My journey wasn't easy, and yours might not be either. But remember, you are never alone. You have the power to change your life, to find your purpose, and to help others along the way. You are stronger than you know, and the world needs what only you can offer. So, take that leap—embrace the unknown. Your dream career, your true calling, is waiting for you on the other side of fear. The setbacks you face today are simply the stepping stones to a brighter, more fulfilling future. Trust that, and keep moving forward. Every obstacle is an opportunity to learn, to grow, and to transform. You have the power to turn every setback into the starting point for your greatest comeback yet. Believe in yourself, and trust that the journey, as difficult as it may be, is leading you exactly where you need to be.

Léonie Rosenstiel

Léonie Rosenstiel's passion for helping people navigate the maze of the elder care system began when she watched several of her relatives become incapacitated. She has spent over 19 years researching guardianship system problems. She writes, speaks, teaches, coaches and is forming a nonprofit. Léonie is the author of *Protecting Mama: Surviving the Legal Guardianship Swamp, Legal Protection: Affordable Options for Individuals, Families, and Small Businesses,* and *They're Coming for Your Elders and Your Inheritance.* She also created the *Dayspring Empowerment Summit* and the *Dayspring Empowerment Course.*

Contact her at: leonie@dayspringresources.com or https://www.linkedin.com/in/leonierosenstiel/

The Music of Life

By Léonie Rosenstiel

"In the depth of winter, I finally learned that within me there lay an invincible summer." —Albert Camus

Sometimes I changed, voluntarily. Other times, I had to be pushed by the universe a little bit to give something up so that I could progress to something new.

I started out as a musician, and of course my hands were very important in that art.

In 1962, When I was going to the pre-college division of Juilliard, I broke a finger on my left hand, in a freak accident. I was a violinist, which made it very, very difficult, but I managed to overcome that.

I had later accidents. When it wasn't possible, physically, to overcome them, some years after that I had to stop playing anyway.

Before that happened, back in 1964, I had already lost a job because I wanted to be a writer and an English major at Barnard College. I had two professors of English during my freshman year who were very much against either musicians going to college at all or musicians trying to write. And so they discouraged me from being a writer. I stayed in college anyway and became a music major instead.

Then, I went across the street. (Columbia University is located across Broadway from Barnard College.) I was accepted as a graduate student in Columbia University's musicology department, and that work was all about writing about music. So I was going to write anyway, and I ended up being an editor for their scholarly musicology journal. I got my Ph.D. from Columbia in 1974. So that was switch number one.

I wrote about music. In 1977, I ended up going to Paris to write the biography of a French musician, a French music teacher by the name of Nadia Boulanger. She had taught all of the major American classical composers of the 20th century.

That was a major switch, because nobody ever expected her to allow anybody to write her biography. But I had written about her sister, Lili, as my doctoral dissertation, and so when I asked her, she said yes, and everyone was shocked.

So this is like going with the flow, knowing what you're interested in, knowing where you want to be, knowing how you want to be there. And that was another switch. It was a very intense experience. For a period of about four years I was going back and forth to Paris. I was meeting all sorts of people. It was a very exciting time, and a very volatile time of changes in my life, changes in what I was doing.

I finished the manuscript, and it surprised me because I had conclusions that my editor wasn't happy with. I found out things, and I said things that she hadn't expected. And so there was a disconnect there and I didn't work further with her. If that was a job, her publishing house did publish the book, but I also lost that job because I never wrote a book for that publisher again.

But the book, *Nadia Boulanger: A LIfe in Music*, was published in 1982. It's still in print, and a few weeks ago, it was optioned for a movie. Things happen in their own good time.

I went into publishing. I had already met my husband, who was a literary agent. And so I worked in his literary agency for a number of years. In 1984, we started putting out a book together, trying to help other writers get published. Literary Agents of North America became a well known reference book in the field, and it went through a number of different editions over a period of more than ten years.

In the late 1980s, I studied at a place in New York called The New Seminary, which was then a school teaching spiritual development, ministry, and interfaith cooperation. I graduated from there and was ordained as a minister in 1990. For seven years, I taught a course at the seminary on spiritual healing.

While I was still involved in the publishing operation with my husband, and still teaching at The New Seminary, I decided that I wanted to learn more about acupuncture and Oriental medicine. And so, in 1993, I went to school for that.

After I graduated from acupuncture college, my husband and I moved to Albuquerque. He wanted to retire and write, and I wanted to practice East Asian medicine.

My mother moved to New Mexico at the same time, but she lived in a separate home. She'd always wanted to live in New Mexico.

In 2003, my mother entered a problematic stage of dementia. My husband had Parkinson's, although we didn't know the name of his illness at the time. He hadn't been properly diagnosed in New York before we moved to New Mexico. At one point they both had dementia at the same time, and it became a difficult balancing act for which I needed all the spiritual healing I could get. I was very grateful that I'd learned this subject well enough to teach it, and could use these techniques for myself when I needed them.

My mother was at the stage of Alzheimer's (some people call it "Stage Four") where people get very volatile and sometimes very combative with the people closest to them. She went into that phase, and at the same time she had harmed herself, and I wanted to protect her. She had almost sliced off a piece of her thumb, hallucinating that she was cutting food because there was no food anywhere near her. I had to grab her and take her quickly down to urgent care to get the thumb stitched up.

I knew then that she couldn't be left alone again. She wanted to be alone in her own house. She really loved being independent, but it's not safe to be independent if you're going to do things that could cause you a lot of grief.

She needed more help. I wanted to become her legal guardian so that I could protect her. Because of the stage of Alzheimer's she was in, she wanted to argue. When I went to court to get the papers, she objected. The judge knew my mother needed a guardian and appointed somebody else. It was a commercial firm.

This resulted in a long and a very painful process for me. At that time they had a theory that, in order for the people who were being taken over by the commercial firm to bond–they called it, "bonding with the Guardian"–they needed to be isolated from the family. For almost 3 years I couldn't see my mother. Once, Mama tried to call, to thank me or the flowers I'd sent her on her birthday. I could hear someone taking the phone out of her hand and hanging it up.

I hurt, emotionally, all that time, and I needed everything I had learned about spiritual healing to get through it.

Meanwhile my husband was sinking deeper and deeper into Parkinson's. I needed to focus on his needs. So I was taking care of Arthur, worrying about my mother, and trying to work at the same time.

My husband passed first, in 2007. Afterward, my attorney managed to convince the Guardian to let me see my mother again. But it was difficult, it was always difficult. They were not friendly and not congenial. I later discovered that there was a belief among the guardians that families were bad for people. Families were harmful, they needed to protect their charges. I don't want to say "wards," but that's what the court calls them. They justified their actions as protecting the wards against their families.

Between 2007 and 2012, I met a lot of people who were in a position similar to mine.

Things got worse for me, because after my mother died in 2012, I was her heir, and I was supposed to be the person administering her estate. They did everything possible to avoid giving me records. I finally had to go to court and subpoena records into the Probate Court to get the information I needed about my mother.

My mother had asked me, after I saw her again, to promise her I'd write about what happened to us. She wanted others to be able to prevent it from happening to them, or mitigate it in some way, because it had been such a terrible experience for her being isolated that way. And it had been a terrible experience for me, too.

The commercial guardian had offered me money, after I saw Mama again, not to speak. The amount of money they offered me kept rising and rising, and eventually it rose to $5 million. Finally, I told them there wasn't any amount of money that they could pay me that would be enough to get me to break my promise to my mother. They really did not like that I'd rejected the money, but I did.

It was 2014. My mother's former guardian and I were opposing each other in a court case, and the judge decided he wanted to officially keep me from speaking. He issued a gag order that forbade me to speak about my mother, forbade me to speak about my family, forbade me to write, forbade me to appear in public, forbade me to talk to my elected officials. In my opinion and in my attorney's opinion, his order violated the First Amendment of the U.S. Constitution.

By then, I'd been writing for many years, and I was a member of the Authors Guild. My attorney and I spoke to the head of the legal department at the Authors Guild. He said that, if we took the case to Federal court, they would give us an amicus brief, and back our argument that it's prior restraint of free speech to prevent someone from speaking and writing that way. Meanwhile, I had that gag order silencing me.

It was so strange, trying to abide by that gag order! After Mama died, and after I inherited her things, there was a piece of textile. It belonged to her and I wanted to frame it. So, here's what happened a few months after the gag order was imposed in 2014:

I walk into a framing shop, bringing the textile with me. The man in the shop says, "Oh, what an interesting piece of textile that is! Who owned it?"

And I answer, "I really can't say."

Is that a strange thing to say to someone or what? He looks at me as if he's thinking, "What planet does this person come from?"

I can't say the word, "mother." I can't say, "my mother." I can't say, "It was my mother's, and I inherited it." I can't say anything.

So the guy is giving me this crazy look.

Meanwhile I had pretty much gone into seclusion because I couldn't talk to people. You can't meet anybody. What do you say to somebody after you first meet them? "Oh, tell me about your family!"

What do you answer? "I can't do it. The court forbids me to." Really? How can you say that?

So I went into seclusion in 2014, and then I learned a lot about how nature heals you, too.

I was pretty much alone except for my wonderfully supportive attorney.

Then, the animals started to come around. I live in Albuquerque, and I have a nice backyard.

Squirrels would bring me fruit and leave it on my back patio. They never did that before. There was a rabbit that did that, too. It was amazing.

You never know where support like that is going to come from, but it's there when you need it. That was a very healing experience, even though living under the gag order was a terrible experience.

The animals rejuvenated me. I felt like a child again, remembering when my parents had a farm in Pennsylvania, during the 1950s. They posted it to prohibit hunting. All the animals seemed to know they were safe there. They'd come into the orchard, and we always left the fruit that fell on the ground there for them. The does would come with their fawns. They'd bring their fawns up to me, and, when I was a little girl, they'd allow me to pet them.

But back to the court case, and to the years 2015-2017. I had journalists calling me, wanting to know about the situation because my friends, whom I couldn't see anymore, had been telling them about this person who was isolated by the court but hadn't done anything wrong. I couldn't even answer them on the phone. I ended up not answering my phone until I saw who was calling because journalists were people the gag order specifically forbade me to speak to. I was not allowed to call back.

Some of the journalists got my email address and would email me, and I would be very, very rude and not answer them. Then, the Albuquerque Journal discovered me.

My attorney had already protested the gag order. The Albuquerque Journal decided it wanted to support that protest because it wanted access to my records and it wanted access to information about my mother.

The Journal couldn't get any documents, and I couldn't use them either, even if I owned them, because there was a very restrictive gag order on the whole thing.

All the hearings relating to my mother had been held in secret over a period of fourteen years. In 2017, when the Albuquerque Journal was present, was the first time other people–people not directly involved in the case–were also sitting in the courtroom. I was told later that the entire first year law class from the University of New Mexico was present at that hearing.

It took a couple of weeks before the judge issued his decision. That was the first time the public was allowed to have knowledge of what was going on. More than one article about my case had already appeared in the paper. Within a couple of weeks after that hearing the judge lifted the gag order, finally lifted it!

I was able to speak again. That year also saw the start of a series of reforms in the State of New Mexico. This was partly due to public interest in my mother's case. There had also been a series of articles about other people who had had a problem with the guardianship of elder loved ones, but it hadn't been as clear that they were being muzzled, gagged, and refused the right to speak. Mine was a very clear-cut case.

There had been some other people who had had orders in their cases that they were not allowed to talk, but the press didn't get involved. I was the one they got involved with, trying to make it possible for me to speak again.

After I was able to write again and publish again, I wrote *Protecting Mama*, the book I'd promised my mother I'd write. It spent a month on an Amazon bestseller list and has now won eighteen awards. I was very, very happy because my mother was a frustrated writer. She had always wanted people, in general, to know about her writing. But she was a college professor, and so the writing that she did was primarily specialized. Other specialists read what she wrote.

I wrote *Protecting Mama*, in a sense, for her as well, but it gave me a whole new career, exposing the problems in the guardianship system and trying to get them solved.

The first book that I showed Jack Canfield, back in 2020, was the manuscript about my mother. I'd given him a much longer draft, and he said that the last third of it was really compelling. He said, "You must develop that." And so I did. That became the book that got all the awards.

After that I realized that one of the problems that a lot of people had, going through the same sort of experience that I did, was that they didn't have access to legal help at the right time, or the right kind of legal help, or from the right person. And so the second book I wrote that Jack saw was *Legal Protection*, a book about protecting yourself legally, and perhaps taking out subscriptions to legal services that can help you along the way.

If you can get advice, anytime you want it, without going broke, the pressure is off. You don't have to deal with the fact that, suddenly there's an emergency, and the feeling of urgency, "I've got to find an attorney right away, because the courts have a deadline."

If you don't have an attorney by the deadline, you don't really know what's going on. They're using words, in court and in documents, but you don't really understand them. You understand what the words mean, out in the everyday world, but you don't understand what the words mean to lawyers and judges.

Jack said he wanted to write the foreword, so he wrote the foreword to that book. It was published in January 2024 and was still on the bestseller list in its category, last I checked.

Now there's *They're Coming for Your Elders*, the next book that I wrote, trying to keep people out of guardianship, and also allow their relatives to have enough money to take care of them.

There was a three-part problem, as I saw it. One was that people don't understand what the ramifications are of this whole situation of having an elder who needs help, and maybe somebody else in your family needs help at the same time, like the problems I experienced with my husband and my mother. A lot of people have that happen when they have teenagers, or 10 or 12 year-olds they need to care for, and then their parents need help at the same time. It happens a lot.

The first part of the solution is knowing what's down the pike for you. The second one is getting good legal advice when you need it, without having to wait, or having to rush out and look for somebody, or going bankrupt in the process. The third one is the monetary piece. You can't care for aging parents if you have only planned your finances so that you can take care of yourself and your children, but no one else. Then, if your parents need help, you can't give it.

And so those three pieces coming together made the last book and Jack wrote the foreword for that one too.

As of this writing, *They're Coming for Your Parents* hasn't been published yet. It just went into the editing process last week, and I'll have my first production conference on it next week.

I could never have predicted where my life path was going to take me, except that it was all about what "resonated" with me at any given time. I gravitate to where the energy resonates.

If you think of resonance being vibrational, and vibration as being a basic component of music, I'm still a musician, and my life is a musical composition. Looking back, I realize that my life has always been about being open, trusting that the path in front of me was the one I needed to take, and letting the energy of discovery carry me where I needed to go.

Jill Eggebraaten

Jill Eggebraaten is a certified life coach, leadership mentor, and trainer with a passion for empowering men to make transformative changes in their lives. As a dynamic speaker and engaging podcaster, Jill reaches a broad audience, providing insightful guidance and actionable advice. With years of experience in coaching and mentoring, she specializes in helping individuals unlock their full potential. Her unique ability to connect with clients on a deep level allows her to effectively support them in overcoming obstacles and achieving their goals.

You can find Jill on her podcast, 'Dude, I got you", or by email at jill@dudeigotyou.com

Change of Plans

By Jill Eggebraaten

"We must let go of the life we have planned, so as to accept the one that is waiting for us." —Joseph Campbell

It was the day before Thanksgiving in my 27th year of marriage, a time that typically brought a flurry of activity in our household. In addition to preparing the feast, I would begin unpacking the Christmas decorations to get a head start for the day after Thanksgiving. I cherished creating a warm and festive atmosphere for our four children, just as my mother had done for me and my five brothers during my childhood. Those moments were truly special to me. However, that 27th year would forever change my perspective on my family and that beloved holiday.

"I want a divorce." Those words felt like they lifted me out of my body. How could this be happening? We don't argue; we communicate, and we still enjoy activities together—don't we? In what felt like just ten seconds, I came to the painful realization that he was right. A wave of emotion hit me, akin to being let go from a job I loved, leaving me with a profound sense of emptiness and overwhelming uncertainty about what lay ahead in my life.

I had already been grappling with the reality that my youngest child would be leaving the nest next year, marking the end of my journey as a full-time mother. This transition into the 'retirement' of motherhood was daunting, especially since it had defined my identity for the past 24 years. I felt incredibly fortunate to have been able to stay home with my children after we moved to Hong Kong, cradling my youngest in my arms while raising the others during our nine years as expatriates. Many women in my position might hesitate to make such a significant change, leaving behind family and everything familiar. Two years earlier, I had lost my mother, who had moved our family five times after leaving the farm in South Dakota with my dad. If she could be brave, why couldn't I?

My life had been dedicated to providing my children with the best possible experiences, and this move felt like an opportunity to do just that.

During my marriage, we moved back to the U.S. from Hong Kong to my hometown of Santa Barbara, CA, and then we embraced new opportunities that took us to Hawaii, Hilton Head, Dubai with three teenagers, back to South Carolina, and finally to Orlando, FL. I viewed each move as an exciting challenge and a chance for the kids to learn about different cultures and the world around them. While change was never easy, it opened up incredible opportunities for our family, and I wholeheartedly supported each transition, guiding the children through the adjustments. My motto during this time was, "Home is where you hang your hat." I often shared this sentiment while working as a Relocation Agent in Hong Kong, helping families navigate what could be one of the biggest changes in their lives.

Over the years of moving, I took on various roles: I was a scout leader, served on the PTA Board, organized fundraisers for scholarships, taught Sunday school, became a master gardener, assisted with the refurbishment of the high school entrance, and worked in the classrooms. I even coached baseball after the head coach told me, "Women make great coaches too." I traveled to colleges and universities as a leadership trainer for my sorority, working with collegians and their advisors. All of these were volunteer positions that allowed me to support the youth and my community. Now, as I face becoming a 'divorcee' I wonder if I'll need to find a real job and what that could possibly be after being out of the workforce for so long. The thought of living alone felt completely overwhelming. How could I turn my skills into a paying job?

Thank goodness I had always been a lifelong learner and recognized that I needed help to discover who I could be after all these changes. The next opportunity came to me in the form of a postcard inviting me to Jack Canfield's "One Day to Greatness" seminar.

Jack is renowned as the co-creator of the *Chicken Soup for the Soul* series, a featured teacher in the film *The Secret*, and America's #1 Success Coach. Walking into that ballroom full of strangers felt like a significant leap, and I was nervous about what might happen. I felt quite vulnerable at that moment and really hoped to avoid an emotional breakdown. Many attendees shared their stories, and I realized that many were experiencing unexpected losses, confusion, and stress about their next steps—just like me. After the seminar, I felt a strange pull to meet Jack. I didn't bring a book for him to sign or a camera for a selfie; I simply introduced myself and expressed my desire to teach others what he had shared. I even boldly added, "Oh, and I'm going to work for you someday!"

Wow, that caught me off guard! Where did that come from— "I'm going to work for you someday?" Since Jack lived in Santa Barbara, maybe my subconscious was suggesting that working with him could be my way back to my hometown, a place where I had experienced so much success and cherished memories. After all, I was the eighth-grade class president, the drill team captain, and I had a wonderful boyfriend in high school. I even landed the lead role in the school play and was accepted to college. Plus, I was one of six chosen nationwide to travel as a leadership trainer for my sorority. Perhaps returning to the place where I felt accomplished and proud of myself was exactly what I needed, rather than feeling discarded after 27 years of working and then being "fired."

Over the following week, I immersed myself in personal development with the Canfield group, earning my training certification to teach Jack Canfield's Success Principles. I attended several more events that provided valuable insights into how I could redirect my life and regain my confidence and focus. I had always been a troubleshooter, and as I mapped out my steps for this new chapter, I felt like I was returning to that role. I took the lead on a few programs, including training as a coach, where I guided participants in identifying areas for change in their lives and helped them take action and stay accountable.

All the work I had done for myself ultimately led me to discover my next calling: coaching.

However, I noticed something intriguing during those years of seminars, workshops, and retreats: there were very few men present. I had spent a significant part of my life surrounded by men—growing up with five older brothers and no sisters. For over 25 years, I served as a Scout leader and trainer for men and youth, and I was the only female coach in the baseball league. Additionally, I supported men through a global weight loss program. I recognized that men could benefit from the knowledge I was gaining. They could learn to strengthen their relationships at work and at home, prioritize self-care, feel more confident in their financial decisions, and take the necessary steps to live their best lives in good health.

They could benefit from what I had learned to build stronger teams at work and enhance the community committees they served on. I understood that they also needed to enjoy life by taking time for fun, especially with their children. I realized it was important for me to focus on working with men specifically, as I had a unique ability to connect with them, earn their trust, and guide them to discover their own answers about what they wanted and how to achieve it. I recognized that many men were facing challenges related to career changes, retirement, and relationships. They needed support just as I did, and now I was equipped to offer that through a coaching program.

Looking back on the past nine years, I can see how often my plans have changed, sometimes with little notice and high hopes, and other times through carefully thought-out steps and significant decisions, often accompanied by anxiety and uncertainty. However, I've come to realize that change is beneficial, truly beneficial. No matter how challenging, change offers the opportunity to create a new life, explore new interests, and discover what you are meant to do. I feel called to guide men through transitions in their lives with individual coaching, addressing the issues that keep them awake at night and helping them move toward their best lives.

Embracing Jack Canfield's *Success Principles*, particularly the idea of "Feel the fear and do it anyway," has brought incredible transformations to my life. Now, in my newfound career, I can help men see and do just that for themselves.

Ryoko Fukui

Ryoko Fukui is a transformational coach guiding women to live authentically, with deep self-love, self-trust, and freedom from traditional paths and self-imposed limits. Originally from Japan, Ryoko felt an urge to break free from societal expectations. Trusting her inner voice, she moved to the U.S., explored Latin America, worked in Mexico, and immigrated to Canada as a newcomer. Pressure to settle into a 9-to-5 in Canada left her feeling misaligned and unfulfilled, leading her to hit rock bottom in 2022. Today, she helps women honor their true desires and build lives aligned with their truth.

Contact info : info@ryokofukui.com
Website : ryokofukui.com

Finding My True Path: From Fear to Freedom

By Ryoko Fukui

"The only way to make sense out of change is to plunge into it, move with it, and join the dance." —Alan Wilson Watts

In the midst of the pandemic's unprecedented pause in 2020, I found myself enveloped in a fog of anxiety, uncertain of what the future held. The world outside was chaotic and unpredictable, but it was the stark realization that I had lost my way and my inner power that truly shook me to my core. For years, I had sought security in external places, my job, my daily routine, having my own place. But as life came to a standstill, those illusions crumbled like dust in the wind. I was adrift, moving through life on autopilot, too afraid to disrupt the status quo. I felt like a ship lost at sea, with no compass to guide me to my true home—my authentic self.

The pandemic stripped away the façade I had carefully constructed over the years since I immigrated to Canada from Japan. I felt trapped, bound by fear, the weight of others' expectations, and the misguided belief that security was found outside myself. I had been conditioned to define success by external markers: financial stability, career advancement, and the approval of those around me. Society constantly fed me the narrative that these were the keys to happiness. Waiting for the right conditions to feel safe became futile, and panic set in as life felt like it was slipping away, like grains of sand through my fingers.

For too long, I had confined myself in a prison of my own making, believing I could control every aspect of my life. I meticulously planned my days, crafted to-do lists, and followed routines as if they were sacred. But the pandemic shattered that illusion. I wasn't in control of the world, nor was I even in control of my own peace of mind. I had been taught that if I had a secure job, worked hard, followed the rules, saved money, and had my own place, I would be rewarded with security. As I sat in the stillness of my home, it became painfully clear that external validation could not fill the void within me. The pandemic revealed a profound truth: security must be created from within.

This realization marked a pivotal turning point in my journey. I knew I needed to embark on a different path, one that required me to confront my fears head-on. I dove into personal development—not as an escape, but as a means of rediscovering my authentic self. I devoured books on mindset, watched countless webinars, and enrolled in courses that promised to unlock my potential. I sought wisdom from authors and speakers who had faced their own struggles and emerged stronger. During this process, I confronted a painful truth: I had lost touch with my true self. I had lived in a victim's mindset, waiting for life to provide answers, unaware that the answers had always resided within me, buried beneath layers of fear and doubt.

Over time and through deep reflection, I began to reclaim my inner power. I started journaling my thoughts and feelings, allowing the words to flow freely onto the page. It became a therapeutic outlet that helped me make sense of the chaos swirling in my mind. I meditated, seeking moments of stillness amidst the noise of the outside world, and embraced practices that quieted the external distractions, allowing me to hear my inner voice more clearly. I engaged in daily affirmations, reminding myself of my worth and capabilities. Slowly but surely, I peeled away the layers of fear and conditioning that had kept me stagnant. I began to see the world through a new lens, one where I realized that no matter what was happening around me, I held the power to create the life I truly desired. It was no longer about mere survival; it was about thriving. It was about reconnecting with my deepest desires and allowing myself to dream again, unfettered by the constraints I had previously imposed upon myself.

During this journey of rediscovery, I began to question everything I once held dear. I reevaluated the long hours I spent at a job that left me feeling empty and unfulfilled. The grind that had once felt like a badge of honor now seemed like a prison sentence. I scrutinized the societal expectations that insisted I play it safe and conform to a mold that never truly fit me. Most importantly, I challenged the belief that I wasn't worthy of more—that my dreams were too big or unrealistic. As I peeled back these layers, a deep yearning emerged within me—a longing to live authentically, in alignment with my true values and desires.

At the beginning of 2023, I decided to leave my comfortable but unfulfilling 9-to-5 job to pursue coaching and training full-time by April 2024. For months, I had been carefully constructing a plan to transition gradually from my job to coaching, taking small, intentional steps toward my dream of inspiring others and guiding them on their journeys to discover what they truly want to do in life and make that dream a reality. Allowing myself this transition period was necessary to avoid risking my financial stability.

However, a pivotal moment forced me to confront my fears head-on. My boss called me, asking me to return to the office after months of remote work. The new location would require an exhausting three-hour commute, making it impossible for me to attend the live calls for my coaching certification—a commitment I had come to view as non-negotiable. Suddenly, the careful balance I had maintained was thrown into disarray. I was faced with a choice: return to the office and hold on to my financial security or fully embrace my dream and risk everything.

This wasn't an easy decision. My job has been my safety net, a source of identity and stability. The thought of letting it go terrified me. What if I failed? What if I wasn't good enough? But something inside me had shifted. I no longer perceived security as external; I had unearthed it within myself. With that newfound clarity, I made the courageous decision to leave, understanding that true security comes from trusting myself.

I informed my boss that I couldn't return, as I needed to follow my new path. So, I chose to quit my job—the security blanket I had held onto for over a decade since immigrating to Canada. The true transformation wasn't in the logistics of my departure but in the inner shift that occurred when I realized I no longer feared losing what I once thought I couldn't live without. I chose to let go of the good to reach for the great.

I sold my condo, letting go of material possessions and the external validations I had clung to for stability. In doing so, I stepped fully into my purpose. This journey was one of letting go—not just of my job and home, but of the old version of myself that believed life was about playing it safe. The more I released, the more space I created for what truly mattered: helping others, connecting with my deepest desires, and living authentically.

Looking back on this chapter of my life, I see that everything unfolded as it was meant to. Losing my job wasn't an ending; it was the beginning of my true path. It taught me that happiness, fulfillment, and security aren't found outside ourselves, they are cultivated within. I had to relinquish the very things I thought I couldn't live without, to uncover the life I was meant to lead. Each step I took, each layer I shed, brought me closer to the woman I was always meant to be.

Now, as a coach and trainer, I dedicate myself to helping other women—especially those feeling confined by societal or cultural expectations—find their own paths. My mission is to empower them to reconnect with their inner strength, to dream boldly, and to live life on their own terms. I understand the struggles they face because I've walked that path myself. My journey wasn't easy, but it was necessary. I learned that sometimes, we must let go of the good to make room for the great, and I'm here to help others do the same.

In Buddhist philosophy, "freedom" means relying on oneself and living according to one's inner truth and wisdom, independent of others or external circumstances. This deep self-understanding leads to true inner freedom. Embracing this concept has shown me that real freedom lies not in fleeing from our fears but in moving through them with confidence and clarity. The journey to inner freedom is not a straight line; it's a winding path filled with ups and downs, but each step brings us closer to our authentic selves.

Stepping into my new role as a coach has transformed not only my career but also my understanding of myself and my life's purpose. I've learned that freedom isn't about avoiding fear; it's about facing it, trusting yourself, and recognizing that you have the power to create a life that resonates with your truth. It's about giving yourself permission to pursue what lights you up, even when the world tells you otherwise.

As you navigate your own journey, remember this: life is always working in your favor, even when it seems like everything is falling apart. Trust in your path. Trust in yourself. Everything you need is already inside you. You have the strength to rise above your circumstances and create a life filled with purpose and passion. Embrace the journey, with all its twists and turns, and know that every step you take is leading you closer to the life you were meant to live.

Terry Deakin

Terry Deakin is a dedicated entrepreneur, career coach, and community leader with 25 years of experience empowering others. From her roots in rural British Columbia, Terry overcame personal challenges to build INEO Employment Services, an organization supporting individuals with employment barriers. Holding a Bachelor of Commerce, an MA in Community Development, and certifications in coaching, she also collaborates with the Chamber of Commerce, Rotary Club, and nonprofits. Passionate about community impact, Terry leads social enterprises focused on environmental sustainability and economic growth. In her free time, she enjoys family, reading, fishing, and camping.

To contact Terry: Email terry@ineoemployment.com or Call +1.250.720.6604

New Beginnings!

By Terry Deakin

"Sometimes quitting is not giving up but making space for new beginnings." —Unknown

When I was a young girl, I dreamed of growing up, getting married, having children, and being a good mom—that would be my job. I graduated from high school with good grades, worked for a year in a group home, and then quit to attend college, enrolling in a Special Care Aide program to work with people living with disabilities. After completing the program, I worked in an institution for about four months before quitting to get married and move for my husband's job. Soon, I had two children—my fairytale life, just what I had always wanted: to be a good mom! But after six years, that dream ended when I left the marriage.

I partied for a while and entered another relationship. Fast forward a few years, and now I'm 32 years old, in my second marriage, with three children—a daughter and two sons. We had a great house and what seemed like the perfect little family. I had two jobs: one, being a good mom, and the other, working as a daycare worker in a private daycare. Everything was going well—lots of friends, kids in school, community involvement—until I made the decision to become a drug addict.

Now, I didn't wake up one day and decide, "I'm going to be a drug addict." I had been using cocaine socially; it was the mid-80s and early 90s, and it was common in certain communities with money and parties—at least in my circles. I learned how to cook cocaine and smoke crack—not the best use of my skills, but new ones nonetheless. Soon enough, my drug use began to interfere with my relationships, family, and community. After a terrible breakup, I moved in with a drug dealer, which made access to drugs all too easy.

Eventually, drugs took over everything. I lost my job and was living on welfare, hitting rock bottom with no clear way out. After about a year and a half of smoking crack and destroying my life, I was on the brink of losing my children. My daughter, who was 13 at the time, said, "Mom, what are you doing? What's going on? You can't let this happen to us!" That was it—the wake-up call I needed. A light bulb switched on. I thought, "What am I doing? This isn't the life I want. This isn't being the good mom I promised myself I'd be."

So, I left the drug dealer and sought counseling. But no one wanted to rent to me or give me a job. Desperate, I got back together with my second husband and moved to a different community.

Here's where things get interesting. The universe provides—we just need to listen. I went to see a drug and alcohol counselor, and when he asked, "What can I do for you?" I burst into tears and said, "I'm a drug addict." He was kind and said, "I don't think you need me, but I know someone you might need." He referred me to a female counselor at the Women's Center. How did he know what I didn't even know about myself?

I soon realized that I was a master of self-sabotage. I never truly believed I deserved the perfect life I had dreamed of. When I was a teenager, I had experienced sexual abuse, but I never told anyone—not my family, not my friends. I shoved it down, locked it away, and let it be my dirty little secret as I moved into adulthood, graduating high school, going to college, getting married, and becoming a mom. But every time I reached a place where I thought I wanted to be, I sabotaged it—my first marriage, my second marriage, everything—because deep down, I didn't believe I deserved love or happiness. Drugs helped me numb that pain and allowed me to live the bad life I thought I deserved.

It wasn't until I heard those five words from my daughter—"Mom, what are you doing?"—that I realized I had to change. I had to start believing in myself if I ever wanted to be successful. Those words, which might be ordinary for many moms, tipped the barrel and woke me up. I am forever grateful to my 13-year-old daughter for saving me.

In recovery, I began being a mom again and started looking for work. I wanted a job working with adults with developmental disabilities, the field I had trained for. Fortunately, the HR person who contacted my previous employer, despite knowing part of my drug use story, decided to give me a chance. I loved working in group homes and soon transitioned to supported employment, helping people with disabilities find and maintain jobs. After a year, I took a leave of absence to go back to college and earn a certificate in human services. That's when I realized I wanted to own my own business.

I didn't know what that would look like at the time, but I knew I had to take responsibility for my life, set goals, and find my path. Then, the universe stepped in again. A Service Canada Program Officer offered the association I worked for a pilot project opportunity called the 'Job Coach Mentor Program,' but the association declined. A coworker suggested, "Terry, why don't we do it? We can write a proposal and apply for the funding ourselves." So, we did. We were successful and asked for leaves of absence from our jobs to try out this pilot project. My coworker's leave was denied, so he quit. I said, "I quit too!" And we started a company called INEO Employment Counseling Inc. INEO, which means 'new beginnings' in Latin, marked a scary but exciting new chapter.

We facilitated the Job Coach Mentor program for about a year and a half before the government cut funding. My business partner sold his share of the company to me for $1 and moved on to become a teacher. I kept the company, securing contracts and writing proposals to grow the business. I wanted to give back, providing 'new beginnings' for people struggling to find work.

As I built the business, I continued my education. At 42, I earned a diploma in Human Services, and at 50, I completed a Bachelor of Commerce, majoring in Entrepreneurship. It was around this time I ended my second marriage. Though it felt like another failure, I knew I had to keep moving forward.

By 2010, I was splitting my time between my company in BC and helping a start-up training school in Alberta. I wasn't looking for a relationship, but the universe had other plans. I found love again and remarried, all while managing my business and returning to university to complete a Master of Arts in Community Development in 2016.

One day, I stumbled across an online course called *Effortless Success* by Jack Canfield, and I was hooked. My husband and I went on a cruise to take a live program with Jack Canfield, and upon returning, I completed his Success Principles Train-the-Trainer program online. Personal and community development became my passion. Helping others build their self-esteem and career paths—what could be better?

In 2019, I founded my first social enterprise—a mattress recycling facility that not only recycled but also provided employment readiness training for people facing barriers. This led to the creation of several other social enterprises: a pet supply store, a woodworking shop, a re-use store, and a recycling depot.

Four years later, I partnered with two amazing people to create a Community Contribution Company, a hybrid for-profit and not-for-profit, focused on community news and event coverage.

My journey has now come full circle. My granddaughter started learning the business a few years ago, and my daughter joined the team last year. The same daughter who once inspired me to change my life is now an excellent career coach, helping others reach their goals.

This past July, as I celebrated 25 years in business, my daughter nominated me for a Career Development Leader of the Year award. This award recognizes an individual who has made a profound impact on the sector, and in September, I learned I was co-recipient of this prestigious title. I am proud to say, "I'm a great leader and a pretty good mom after all!"

As I continue pursuing the work I love—empowering others to build their own paths to success—I am often deeply moved by the stories I hear. Recently, after presenting INEO's mission to a group of students and teachers, a teacher shared something that touched my heart. They paraphrase a parent's words, "INEO saved them, and that's why they're here today with their young adult, enrolling them in one of your programs." It's truly amazing to witness the growth of so many individuals.

Focusing on building my legacy and transitioning leadership to my daughter and granddaughter, but not yet ready to retire, I am truly living my passion by expanding my career coaching to support women across North America who are seeking to live their passion, *New Beginnings: Coaching with Terry Deakin*.

Leona Burton

Leona Burton is a dynamic entrepreneur, advanced Jack Canfield Trainer, and the visionary CEO of MIB International. Passionate about empowering women, she has built a global community that supports moms and women in business through training, education, and child-friendly networking. With her signature blend of expertise and authenticity, Leona inspires others to achieve success while balancing the beautiful chaos of life and motherhood.

You can contact me at Leona@mibint.co

You Are Enough: Rebuilding After Losing It All

By Leona Burton

"Success isn't about how much money you make; it's about the difference you make in people's lives." —Michelle Obama

My Journey from Loss to Purpose

It took losing everything to truly find myself. When I walked away from a multi-million-pound business, leaving behind a team, bank account, and future that once seemed secure, I didn't just lose my job, I lost my identity. Yet, that moment became the foundation of a journey toward self-discovery, resilience, and, ultimately, success on my own terms.

The day I decided to leave was like watching a dream shatter. My business partner and I had built something extraordinary: we were featured in Forbes, appeared on television, and received offers for radio shows and production deals. Then, within days, it all disappeared, and I was left with no business, no team, no resources, nothing. I spent that weekend mourning everything I'd lost. But on Monday, I knew I couldn't stay in that place. I had to rebuild from scratch, and this time, it would be on my terms.

Before this business, I'd already faced hardship. After a successful seven-year career in television, I chose to step back to care for my son, who had recently been diagnosed with autism. Starting a business felt like the right move, though I knew little about entrepreneurship. Within a year, I found myself deep in debt, facing bailiffs at my door, fearing that my young children might lose even the basic comforts of home. Looking back, those early struggles were a blessing in disguise. They taught me resilience and tenacity—qualities that would carry me through when I had to start over years later.

This second beginning was tough. Without my former partner, I had to face the things I excelled at and those I didn't. I was suddenly responsible for every decision, every step forward. Business is hard enough, but navigating it alone is another level of challenge. At times, the loneliness felt overwhelming. I'd lost the person I'd relied on, and it felt like a personal divorce. But through this experience, I began to understand what I wanted my business and my life to look like.

Starting over in the middle of COVID-19 was another level of difficulty. But the pandemic also created space for reflection. What was truly important? What kind of business did I want to build? I focused on aligning my values, forming a team that shared my vision, and developing a culture of integrity and strength. I looked back on the person I'd been and realized how much I'd grown through my trials. This new chapter was about more than just financial success, it was about building something sustainable and deeply meaningful.

What I learned from these challenges is that every setback, no matter how devastating, is temporary. Success is temporary. Failure is temporary. When we start viewing our experiences this way, we find the strength to push through. Today, whenever I encounter a roadblock, I draw on past struggles to remind myself, "I've overcome before, and I can do it again." I believe that resilience comes from facing life head-on. Avoiding challenges only delays growth, while confronting them teaches us who we truly are.

Through my journey, I've come to understand that we each hold the power to lift others up. We don't need monumental success to make an impact. By sharing our authentic selves, by listening deeply, we find shared experiences that connect us. When we open up without shame or fear, we build bridges that can transform lives. In a world where so many are struggling, there's power in knowing we aren't alone.

The most valuable lesson I've learned is that I am enough. We often feel driven to seek the next accomplishment or connection, thinking it will make us whole. But we're already complete. Everything we've survived, all the lessons we've learned, has brought us to this moment. Yes, it's okay to pursue new goals and challenges, but it's also essential to pause and recognize our own strength. We've endured. We've grown. And that's worth celebrating.

My journey from loss to rediscovery wasn't easy. It's taken grit, resilience, and a willingness to believe in myself again. To anyone reading this who may be facing their own challenges, remember this: You are enough. Right here, right now, with all your skills, experiences, and strengths. Life will continue to challenge you, but each trial is another step in your transformation. And as you move forward, remember to look within and recognize the incredible person you already are.

Epilogue

To our dear readers: as you close the pages of *I Quit! - How to Lose Your Job and Find Your Dream Career, I* hope you carry with you a renewed sense of purpose and possibility.

You may have picked up this book feeling uncertain, discouraged, or even broken by the weight of job loss or career dissatisfaction. Perhaps you saw a reflection of yourself in the authors' struggles—the fear of an uncertain future, the vulnerability of starting over, or the courage to dream beyond what seems possible. Whatever brought you here, know this: you are not alone.

Through these stories, we have shared diverse journeys, some marked by clarity and determination, others by the exploration of unknown passions or the serendipity of chance. Each story was written with you in mind, to remind you that job loss or career reinvention isn't a failure, but a chance to pivot and grow.

You don't necessarily have to leave your current job to make a change. Instead, you can find ways to transform it into a meaningful career—or even a calling. This is your opportunity to redefine what success means to you, to align your work with your values, and to uncover a path that brings true fulfillment and joy.

The world is undergoing an extraordinary transformation. The pandemic and the "Great Resignation" have prompted many of us to reevaluate our priorities and redefine success on our terms. These stories resonate because they are real. They are about people like you—people who stumbled, fell, and ultimately found the strength to rise again. They illustrate that career transitions are not linear, and sometimes, the best paths are the ones we never planned.

As you turn the final page, I invite you to take one step today—no matter how small—toward building your dream career. Ask yourself:

What do I truly want? What lights me up? Let these stories inspire you to dream boldly and take action.

Reflect on the Japanese concept of *ikigai*, which means "reason for being." It's the intersection of four essential elements: ***What you are good at. What you love. What you can be paid for. What the world needs.***

Use this framework as a guide to discovering your unique path. Think about how your passions, skills, and values can come together to create a fulfilling career that serves not just yourself, but the world around you. Let these stories inspire you to dream boldly, explore deeply, and take action with intentionality.

Your journey may not look like anyone else's, and that's the beauty of it. Success is not a destination but a path you carve with resilience, heart, and purpose. You hold the pen to your own story. Write it well and let your *ikigai* light the way.

To our readers who supported this initiative, your purchase goes beyond fostering personal growth, it also contributes to a meaningful cause. By supporting the victims of Hurricanes Helene and Milton, you've shown that transformation and generosity can create ripples of positive change and a legacy of hope and resilience.

Please Post a Review

If this book has inspired you or touched your heart, I would greatly appreciate your review. Share what stood out to you—whether it was a story of resilience, a fresh perspective on career reinvention, or a spark of motivation for you to create your dream career.

Your feedback and insights not only support the authors, but can also encourage others to explore these powerful stories and find their own path to growth and transformation.

Thank you for being part of this mission to inspire, share hope and uplift others in times of need around the world!

Get linked to post a review on Amazon:
https://www.globaltransformation.life/book-review

Or scan the QR code:

Printed in Great Britain
by Amazon

57611375R00099